ACT
EXAM PREP

The Most Complete Guide to Passing the Exam on Your First Try with the Highest Score | Includes 6 Full Exam Simulations and EXTRA Weekly Exams Based on the New ACT Format

BY JASON PERLE

Table of contents

HERE IS YOUR FREE BONUS:

Additional Exam Simulations, ONE EACH WEEK

Maximize your ACT test performance with exclusive, no-cost extras unlock them with the link or the QR code provided.

Embark on the path to ACT mastery with our expertly crafted, free supplementary materials available for instant download. Tailored to enhance your comprehension and test-taking prowess, these indispensable resources are your key to attaining unparalleled preparedness.

CLICK HERE TO DOWNLOAD IT

OR

SCAN THE QR CODE TO DOWNLOAD IT

PREFACE

Welcome to your comprehensive guide to conquering the ACT!
Preparing for the ACT is a journey that extends beyond simple mastery of high school subjects. For many students it represents a gateway to their future, whether that means gaining admission to a preferred college, securing scholarships, or even just proving to themselves that they are ready for the next academic challenge. However, the significance of the ACT can often make the process feel overwhelming. This test, with its rigid time constraints and demanding questions, can become a source of anxiety for students who feel the pressure to perform well not only for themselves but also for their families and future aspirations.

When we approach test preparation, it's important to acknowledge the emotional aspect as well. Many students carry the weight of expectations, both internal and external, when they begin studying. They may worry about disappointing their families or fear that they are not capable of achieving the scores needed for their dream schools. It's easy to get caught up in comparisons, watching peers score higher or reach their goals more quickly, and this can lead to feelings of inadequacy. But it's essential to remember that every student's journey is different, and that success on the ACT comes down to preparation, persistence, and mindset rather than innate ability.

One of the most important shifts you can make as you begin your ACT prep is to focus on the process rather than the outcome. It's natural to fixate on the final score you hope to achieve, but thinking too much about the outcome can lead to unnecessary pressure. Instead, concentrate on the daily steps you can take to improve. Every practice test, every section you review, brings you closer to your goal. This exam is not a test that measures intelligence or potential, it's a test that evaluates how well you've prepared… and preparation is something you can control.

As you prepare, keep in mind that the ACT rewards consistency. It's not about cramming all the knowledge into your brain at once; it's about building a strong foundation of understanding over time. Setting up a regular study schedule, where you tackle small pieces of the exam day by day, is the most effective way to retain information and improve your test-taking skills. Think of your ACT prep as a marathon rather than a sprint. The students who succeed are often the ones who pace themselves, approach their study sessions strategically, and stay committed over the long term.

Beyond the content itself, one of the biggest hurdles for many students is test anxiety. It's perfectly normal to feel nervous when faced with a high-stakes test like this, but learning how to manage that anxiety is key. Remember that nerves can be transformed into energy that drives you forward rather than holds you back. Practice mindfulness techniques like deep breathing or visualization to help calm your mind before and during the test. Reassure yourself that it's okay to make mistakes during practice, and use those mistakes as learning opportunities to adjust your approach.

In preparing for the exam remember that you are not defined by a number. This test, while important, is just one component of your college application. It's a tool that helps admissions officers gauge your readiness for college-level work, but it doesn't encapsulate who you are as a student or a person. Your work ethic, determination, and resilience are what truly matter, and these qualities will shine through in everything you do, whether it's on test day or beyond.

Finally, believe in yourself. ACT preparation can be daunting, but with the right strategies and mindset, you have the power to succeed. The journey may have its ups and downs, but each step brings you closer to achieving your goals. Trust the process, put in the effort, and know that you're capable of far more than you realize. Let's get started!

Chapter 1: Introduction to the ACT

What's New in the ACT (2025 Edition)

One of the most notable updates is the test's shortened duration. Previously lasting about three hours, the ACT will now take roughly two hours to complete. This reduction in time is not only intended to lessen student fatigue but also to make the exam a more streamlined experience. Students often cite the length of the test as a source of stress, and this adjustment should help reduce the mental strain that can build up over longer exams. Shorter testing times also make the test-taking experience more practical for students who may have packed schedules filled with extracurriculars, jobs, or other academic commitments.

Another significant update involves the number of questions. The total has been reduced from 215 to 171, meaning students will now have fewer questions to answer in each section. While this could seem like a minor change, it impacts the test-taking experience in a meaningful way. Fewer questions give students more time to consider each one carefully, allowing for deeper focus and minimizing the rush to complete each section. Historically, the ACT has been known for its fast-paced nature, where managing time has often been one of the biggest challenges for students. The new format allows for slightly more breathing room, giving students an opportunity to apply the strategies they've learned more effectively without feeling excessively pressed for time.

The revised ACT also reflects a shift in its core structure. While it has long consisted of English, Math, Reading, and Science sections, the Science section will now be optional. This change mirrors the optional Writing section, which has been in place for several years. For many students, this added flexibility will be a welcome relief, especially for those whose strengths lie in English or Math and who may not wish to demonstrate proficiency in scientific reasoning. However, it's important to note that students planning to apply to competitive STEM programs may still need to take the Science section, as it could be required for certain college admissions or scholarships.

The test's availability in both paper and online formats remains an important aspect of its accessibility. Some students feel more comfortable with traditional paper-based exams, while others may prefer the convenience of taking the test digitally. The continued choice between these two formats reflects an understanding that students have different preferences and test-taking strengths. It's worth noting that while online testing will be available at select locations, not all test centers will offer it, so students should be mindful when registering.

While the ACT is adopting these updates the test's core purpose remains unchanged. It is still a tool designed to assess a student's readiness for college-level work. The changes are intended to reduce unnecessary barriers and provide a more focused, manageable experience. These updates reflect ACT's commitment to making the test both rigorous and fair, ensuring it continues to serve as a valuable metric in college admissions without overwhelming the students who take it.

Overview of the shorter test format - 2 hours for 171 questions-

The upcoming changes to the ACT, effective from spring 2025, include a significant adjustment to the test's length, reducing it to roughly two hours. This shortened format, paired with a reduction in the total number of questions to 171, is designed to streamline the testing experience and address concerns about the mental fatigue that often accompanies longer exams. The new format is more focused, giving students the opportunity to dedicate more time and attention to each question without the overwhelming pressure of a three-hour commitment.

The decision to shorten the exam reflects a growing awareness of the importance of mental stamina in test performance. Previously, the ACT's three-hour length often left students feeling drained, particularly toward the end of the test. As the final sections approached, focus and accuracy could suffer, not necessarily due to a lack of knowledge, but rather because of the cumulative mental exhaustion that builds during a prolonged exam. The reduced two-hour format mitigates this issue, helping students maintain their concentration and sharpness from start to finish.

The new format of 171 questions, compared to the previous 215, will naturally have a significant impact on how students approach each section. With fewer questions overall, students will no longer need to rush through sections as quickly as before. One of the most frequently cited challenges of the ACT in its current form is its fast-paced nature, where students often feel the pressure to move through questions rapidly to ensure they have enough time to complete each section. The updated format offers more breathing room, allowing students to focus more deeply on each question.

The time-per-question ratio is one of the most crucial aspects of this shorter format. In the past, students were given limited time to process and respond to questions, particularly in sections like Reading and Science, which involve interpreting data and making inferences. With the new structure, students will have more time to engage with each question. For instance, the English section, which has traditionally required students to answer 75 questions in 45 minutes, will now contain 50 questions in 35 minutes. Similarly, the Math section will feature 45 questions in 50 minutes, compared to the previous 60 questions in 60 minutes. This change gives students a few extra seconds per question, which might not seem like much but can make a significant difference in alleviating the time pressure.

The introduction of fewer, more targeted questions also enhances the precision of the test. The ACT aims to measure critical skills and knowledge without overwhelming students with excessive content. This refinement means that students must be prepared to answer thoughtfully and deliberately, rather than relying on a volume of questions to balance out the difficulty. The focus on fewer but more impactful questions encourages students to understand the core concepts being tested, making their preparation more meaningful and efficient.

In essence, the ACT's shorter, more concise format for 2025 reflects an understanding of the evolving needs of students. It aligns with a broader trend in standardized testing, where efficiency and clarity are prioritized. While the test remains a challenging measure of college readiness, this new structure ensures that students can approach it with less exhaustion and more focus, ultimately leading to a more positive testing experience. The balance of fewer questions and more time per question provides a fairer and more manageable environment, helping students showcase their skills and knowledge without being overwhelmed by the clock.

Science section now optional, Core focus on English, Reading and Math

Starting in the spring of 2025, the ACT will make its Science section optional, a significant shift in the structure of the test. This change is part of a broader update designed to give students more flexibility in how they demonstrate their readiness for college-level academics. The core sections of the exam—English, Reading, and Math—will now serve as the primary focus, while the Science and Writing sections will be optional add-ons. This adjustment reflects an evolving perspective on standardized testing, one that aims to reduce unnecessary pressures while maintaining a rigorous assessment of essential academic skills.

For many students, the Science section of the ACT has long been viewed as one of the most challenging parts of the test. It demands not only knowledge of scientific concepts but also the ability to interpret data quickly, make inferences from graphs and charts, and compare conflicting viewpoints. By making this section optional, the ACT gives students greater control over how they present their academic strengths. This is particularly beneficial for students whose academic interests do not align closely with the sciences, allowing them to focus on areas where they feel more confident, like math or reading comprehension.

However, the Science section will still play a crucial role for students aiming for certain academic tracks, particularly those interested in STEM fields. For applicants to highly competitive engineering, pre-med, or scientific research programs, opting into the Science section will likely remain important. These students will need to demonstrate not only their abilities in English, Math, and Reading but also their proficiency in interpreting and analyzing scientific data. Colleges and universities with strong STEM programs may continue to look for science scores to gauge applicants' readiness for rigorous coursework in these fields.

The decision to shift the Science section to an optional component also brings the ACT more in line with other standardized tests, like the SAT, which does not have a dedicated science section. The ACT's Science section has always set it apart from the SAT, and now students applying to schools that accept either test will face a more similar testing experience, which may allow for easier comparisons between scores.

In terms of preparation, students will need to consider their academic goals and the requirements of the colleges they are applying to when deciding whether to take the Science section. For those who feel confident in their data interpretation and scientific reasoning skills, the Science section could be an opportunity to further boost their composite score and demonstrate their analytical abilities. On the other hand, students who are applying to programs that don't require science proficiency may find it advantageous to focus their energy on excelling in the core subjects of English, Math, and Reading, where their efforts will have the most impact.

Overall, the shift toward making the Science section optional reflects the ACT's broader focus on flexibility and personalization. Students are being given more choice in how they present their strengths, and this change is particularly meaningful for those whose academic paths don't require a strong focus on scientific reasoning. By reducing the required sections, the ACT aims to balance rigor with a more student-centered approach, making the test more adaptable to individual learning profiles and career aspirations.

What to expect: Paper vs. online testing

One of the most notable changes coming with the 2025 ACT update is the increased flexibility in how students can take the test: they will now have the option to take it either on paper or online. This choice is designed to accommodate different preferences and test-taking styles, while ensuring that the ACT remains accessible to a wide range of students. Both formats offer the same content, difficulty level, and scoring system, but they differ in terms of user experience, preparation, and logistics. Understanding what to expect from both options is essential for students to make an informed decision.

The paper-based format remains the traditional method for taking the ACT. Many students are accustomed to this style of testing, having experienced similar formats throughout their school years. The familiarity of bubbling in answers with a pencil, having a physical booklet to mark up, and pacing oneself without the distraction of a computer screen can feel more comfortable to students who prefer a tactile experience. The paper test allows students to easily skip around, underline passages, and take notes in the margins—all methods that can help with focus and comprehension.

However, the paper test also comes with some limitations. Time management is often more challenging in a paper format, as students need to flip back and forth between the test booklet and the answer sheet, and they don't have the benefit of a built-in timer. Additionally, for students with messy handwriting or who tend to misalign their answers with the wrong question numbers, the paper format can introduce risks of mistakes. Despite these challenges, many students feel more in control and less distracted when using paper.

The online format, on the other hand, offers a more modern, tech-driven experience. Students who are comfortable with computers may find the online test to be more intuitive and easier to manage in terms of timing. The online format includes built-in tools, such as timers and highlighters, which can help students keep track of time and focus on key information without needing to flip pages or manually check the clock. Moreover, the digital interface allows for quick navigation between questions, and the answer choices are directly tied to each question, reducing the risk of misalignment errors.

One potential advantage of the online format is the ability to test in an environment that mirrors the increasing use of digital tools in higher education. As more colleges and universities transition to online learning platforms, becoming comfortable with digital testing may help students feel more prepared for the kinds of assessments they will encounter in college. However, the online format does require students to be comfortable reading on a screen for extended periods, which can be tiring for some, particularly when compared to reading from a physical page. Screen fatigue can be a challenge, and those who are not accustomed to digital reading may find it more difficult to focus.

For students who live in areas where reliable internet access or technical support may be limited, the paper format may still be the more practical option. It is important to note that while the online version offers conveniences, it is not available at every testing location, so students who prefer this option need to ensure that it is offered at their chosen test center.

In deciding between paper and online, students should consider their comfort with technology, their ability to focus on a screen versus a physical page, and the logistics of the testing center. Ultimately, both formats are designed to assess the same skills, and the choice should come down to which environment will best help the student perform confidently and efficiently.

Why the test changed and how to use these changes to your advantage

The changes to the ACT, coming into effect in the spring of 2025, were designed in response to the evolving landscape of standardized testing and the educational environment in general. These adjustments reflect a recognition that both students and educators have expressed concerns over the previous format, particularly regarding its length and the time pressure it placed on test-takers. By shortening the exam, reducing the number of questions, and making the Science section optional, the ACT is adapting to meet the needs of today's students while maintaining its rigor as a college admissions tool. Understanding why these changes were made, and how to use them to your advantage, is crucial for getting the most out of your ACT preparation.

One of the primary reasons for the change is the issue of student fatigue. Historically, the ACT was a marathon-like experience, stretching for three hours and requiring sustained concentration. Many students reported that the sheer length of the test contributed to mental exhaustion, which often affected performance, especially toward the end of the exam. The shortened format, now about two hours, aims to alleviate this issue. With fewer questions and a reduced testing time, students are better positioned to maintain focus throughout the entire exam, leading to more consistent performance. As a test-taker, this means you can now approach each section with the energy needed to tackle difficult questions without feeling drained by the middle of the test.

In addition to fatigue, time pressure was a significant issue with the previous format. Many students felt rushed to complete sections, leading to hasty mistakes, skipped questions, and a general sense of panic. The reduction in the total number of questions (171 instead of 215) gives students more time per question, offering a chance to slow down and focus on accuracy rather than simply racing against the clock. This is a valuable change, and students should capitalize on it by honing their time-management skills. Use practice tests to familiarize yourself with the new pacing and build strategies that allow you to maximize the time available for each question, especially in the more challenging sections like Math and Reading.

The decision to make the Science section optional also reflects the changing priorities in college admissions. For many years, the Science section was one of the defining features that distinguished the ACT from other standardized tests. However, not all students plan to pursue STEM fields, and many found the Science section particularly challenging or irrelevant to their intended academic paths. By making it optional, the ACT now allows students to focus on the core areas (English, Reading, and Math) that are most relevant to their strengths and college goals. If you're not aiming for a science-based degree, you can use the extra time and energy to refine your performance in these core sections. On the other hand, if you plan to pursue a STEM-related career, you can still opt in for the Science section and demonstrate your proficiency in that area.

The changes to the ACT reflect a broader shift toward student-centered testing. By offering flexibility in test formats (both paper and online) and allowing students more control over which sections to take, the ACT is acknowledging the diverse needs of test-takers. This gives students the opportunity to customize their test-taking experience in ways that best align with their strengths. The key to leveraging these changes is to assess your own academic profile, understand which sections will best highlight your abilities, and practice accordingly.

In summary, the changes are meant to reduce stress, allow for greater flexibility, and ensure that students can demonstrate their abilities without unnecessary obstacles. To use these changes to your advantage, focus on improving time management, choose the sections that best align with your academic goals, and take full advantage of the flexibility offered by the new format.

Chapter 2: The First Step – Mastering Time Management and Strategy

Understand new time constraints

As of 2025, the new format of the exam introduces revised time constraints that students must fully understand to perform their best. With the overall testing time reduced from three hours to approximately two, along with a reduction in the total number of questions, students will now experience a shift in how they manage their time during the exam. These changes, while designed to reduce fatigue and stress, also require a thoughtful approach to ensure that students can efficiently use the time provided to maximize their scores.

The first thing to note is the impact of these new constraints on time-per-question. Previously, the test was known for its fast-paced nature, forcing students to move quickly from one question to the next, often with little room to pause and reflect. In the updated format, with 171 questions instead of 215, students now have a bit more time to devote to each one. This slight increase in available time per question is particularly significant because it allows for a more thoughtful approach to answering, reducing the pressure to rush through sections.

For instance, in the English section, students will have 35 minutes to answer 50 questions. This translates to approximately 42 seconds per question. In comparison to the previous format, where students had only slightly more time but a greater number of questions, this adjustment makes it easier to manage the section without feeling overwhelmed by the clock. Students who previously struggled with the time limits in English now have more room to breathe and focus on accuracy.

Similarly, in the Math section, the 50-minute time limit applies to 45 questions, providing approximately one minute and seven seconds per question. This is a modest but impactful increase in time compared to the previous format, where students had 60 questions to complete in 60 minutes. For many students, Math has been a section where time management is particularly challenging, especially for more complex problems that require multiple steps to solve. The extra time here will allow students to carefully consider their approach to each problem, reducing careless errors caused by rushing.

The Reading section sees a similar adjustment, with students now having 40 minutes to answer 36 questions. This works out to about one minute and seven seconds per question, offering more breathing room compared to the previous version, which often felt rushed, especially for students who take longer to process dense passages. This additional time allows for deeper engagement with the material, ensuring students can more thoughtfully analyze and respond to the questions without the panic of running out of time.

Understanding these new time constraints is key to adapting your test-taking strategy. The slight increase in time per question doesn't mean students should get too comfortable, though. While there's more room for focus and accuracy, the test still demands efficient decision-making. Practicing under timed conditions will remain essential, and students should focus on building both speed and precision in their responses. Mock tests and practice sessions can help solidify pacing, ensuring that you use the time advantage wisely without lingering too long on any one question.

Lastly, the optional Science section, if chosen, offers a similar benefit of additional time per question. With 40 minutes to complete 40 questions, students have approximately one minute per question, allowing them to thoroughly analyze data, graphs, and scientific information without feeling as rushed.

In conclusion, the revised time constraints provide a balance of more focus per question while still maintaining the overall rigor of the test. The key is to understand how this affects your pacing in each section, to make the most of the additional time, and to ensure that you remain focused and efficient throughout. With the right preparation and an understanding of these new limits, you can use the time available to your full advantage.

How to identify high-value questions quickly

In any standardized test, one of the most important strategies for maximizing your score is learning how to quickly identify and prioritize high-value questions. While the new exam format offers more time per question, time management remains critical. Not all questions are created equal, and knowing which ones to tackle first can make a significant difference in your overall performance. The goal is to answer as many questions as accurately as possible within the time limit, and to do so, you must be strategic in identifying which questions to prioritize and which to save for later.

The first step in prioritizing questions is recognizing your own strengths and weaknesses. Some questions will play directly into your areas of strength, while others may challenge you in subjects you find more difficult. Being aware of this early on allows you to capitalize on the questions that you can answer both accurately and quickly, without getting bogged down by more challenging ones right away. For example, if you're strong in algebra but find geometry more difficult, you can quickly answer algebra questions in the Math section first, securing those points before moving on to the more time-consuming or confusing problems. The same goes for other sections, if you know grammar and punctuation rules well, prioritize those in the English section before tackling questions on sentence structure or rhetoric.

Next, it's important to scan the section before diving into the first question. Spending the first minute quickly glancing through the set of questions gives you a general sense of difficulty and allows you to locate questions that seem familiar or straightforward. By identifying easier questions first, you can start gaining momentum, building confidence, and securing points without spending too much time early in the section. This scanning process should be swift, but it's a critical step in building a strategy for each section of the test.

Another effective technique is to triage questions based on complexity and the time they'll likely require. Some questions can be answered almost immediately, these are often direct fact-based or calculation-based questions. These should be prioritized, as they allow you to accumulate points without expending much mental energy. More complex or multi-step questions, on the other hand, should be marked and revisited later if time allows. The trick is not to get stuck on a question simply because it appears early in the test or because you feel you "should" know the answer. Remember, each question typically holds equal weight, so it's wiser to leave the difficult ones for later rather than wasting time and risking missing easier questions toward the end.

In the Reading and Science sections, prioritization becomes especially important because these sections often involve interpreting data or reading passages. In these cases, you might prioritize questions that deal with explicit details, those that can be answered by quickly locating information within the passage or chart. In contrast, inference questions or those that require synthesis of multiple pieces of information are more time-consuming and can be returned to after you've tackled the more straightforward questions.

It's also valuable to employ guessing strategies effectively. If you encounter a particularly tough question, rather than spending unnecessary time on it, make an educated guess and move on. Mark the question so that if time permits, you can revisit it later, but never let one challenging question consume valuable minutes that could be spent answering questions you know well.

Practice is essential for mastering this prioritization process. The more practice tests you take, the better you'll become at quickly identifying high-value questions and refining your approach. Over time, you'll develop an intuitive sense of which questions deserve immediate attention and which can be left for the end. This skill, learning how to prioritize questions and manage your time, can make a significant difference in both your confidence and your final score, helping you navigate the exam more efficiently and effectively.

Building a strategic mindset

Developing a strategic mindset is one of the most critical components of test success. This is especially true for timed exams, where efficiency and focus are essential. One key strategy that many students overlook is learning to concentrate on the questions they know well, while skipping those that seem difficult or time-consuming, with the intention of returning to them later. By adopting this approach, you avoid wasting valuable time, increase your chances of answering more questions correctly, and reduce the mental strain that can occur when you get stuck.

The first step in building this mindset is to focus on what you know. In any section of a test, there will be questions that you can answer confidently and quickly. These are your high-value opportunities, and prioritizing them ensures you maximize your score in the areas where you're strongest. When you approach a question that feels familiar or involves a concept you're comfortable with, tackle it immediately. This boosts your confidence early on, helping you build momentum and alleviate the anxiety that can accompany challenging questions. Furthermore, these questions usually require less mental energy, allowing you to save your brainpower for tougher ones later on.

Skipping questions you don't know right away can feel counterintuitive at first. Many students fall into the trap of dwelling on difficult questions, thinking that they need to conquer every problem in the order it appears. However, this approach can significantly harm your performance. When you hit a particularly challenging or unfamiliar question, it's easy to spend too much time struggling with it, which can lead to panic or frustration. That, in turn, affects your performance on the questions that follow. The smarter approach is to mark these difficult questions, skip them, and come back to them at the end if time allows.

Skipping doesn't mean abandoning a question entirely. The goal is to keep moving forward, answering as many questions as you can with confidence, and returning later when you've completed the rest of the section. By doing this, you ensure that you don't miss out on easier points that you could have gained elsewhere. This technique is especially helpful in subjects like Math and Reading, where questions can vary in difficulty. A question that stumps you initially may feel more manageable after you've answered other questions and gained a better sense of the section's overall flow.

Another advantage of this strategy is the mental reset it provides. When you return to a question after completing the section, you're often seeing it with fresh eyes and a clearer perspective. Sometimes the break can allow your brain to process information in the background, or even jog a memory that wasn't immediately accessible when you first encountered the question. You may also notice patterns or details that you missed earlier, simply because you were less stressed and better able to focus.

Of course, this strategy requires discipline and practice. It's tempting to dwell on a tough question because we all want to feel like we've solved everything. But the reality is that tests are not about perfection—they're about maximizing points within a limited time. By adopting a mindset that encourages you to move through the test efficiently and avoid getting stuck, you will become a much more effective test-taker.

To implement this strategy successfully, it's crucial to practice under timed conditions. The more you expose yourself to the rhythm of the test, the easier it becomes to identify which questions you know well and which ones can be set aside for later. By building this strategic mindset, you'll be able to approach the exam with confidence, knowing that you can manage your time effectively and prioritize the questions that will lead to your success.

How to handle multiple-choice answers

One of the key changes in the Math section of the revised 2025 test format is the reduction of answer choices from five to four. This shift might seem small at first glance, but it brings with it a few strategic implications that can greatly benefit test-takers. Understanding how to handle multiple-choice questions effectively in this new format is essential for maximizing your score and approaching the section with confidence.

The most immediate impact of reducing the number of answer choices is that it increases the odds of guessing correctly when you are unsure of the answer. Previously, with five answer choices, the probability of guessing the correct answer stood at 20%, or 1 in 5. With the new four-answer format, however, your odds improve to 25%, or 1 in 4. While guessing should never be your first strategy, having a higher chance of guessing correctly makes educated guessing a more effective fallback when you're pressed for time or unsure about a particular question. This is especially useful when you can confidently eliminate one or two answer choices, narrowing down the field even further.

But improved guessing odds are only one part of the equation. The four-answer format also encourages a more strategic approach to eliminating incorrect answers. In many cases, even if you're not entirely sure of the correct answer, you can quickly identify at least one or two options that are clearly wrong. This could be due to an obvious miscalculation in a numerical answer or a conceptual error that contradicts the principles of the problem. By practicing this elimination technique, you can significantly increase your chances of choosing the correct answer from the remaining options, even if you aren't entirely certain of it.

With fewer answer choices, students may also find it easier to manage their mental stamina throughout the test. One of the challenges of multiple-choice tests is the cognitive load involved in weighing each option carefully. With four options instead of five, you are required to process slightly less information per question, which can help you sustain focus as you work through the Math section. This reduction in cognitive load, though subtle, can make a difference over the course of 45 questions, helping to reduce decision fatigue and making the test feel a bit more manageable.

Another important consideration is that the structure of the questions themselves may evolve to reflect the four-answer format. The reduction in answer choices could allow for more nuanced or complex questions, as there are fewer answers to distract from the correct one. This means that while the odds of guessing correctly increase, so too might the difficulty of some of the questions, especially those that require multiple steps to solve. Therefore, it's crucial that you focus on strengthening your core math skills to avoid relying too much on guessing and to ensure that you can confidently answer the questions that fall within your areas of strength.

One way to adjust to the four-answer format is to practice using materials that mimic this new structure. By working through problems that offer four choices, you can fine-tune your ability to quickly evaluate the given options and make more efficient decisions. Additionally, practicing under timed conditions will help you balance the need to move swiftly through the section with the ability to eliminate incorrect answers and make educated guesses when necessary.

This change also emphasizes the importance of test-taking discipline. With fewer answer choices, it might be tempting to rush through questions, thinking that it will be easier to spot the correct answer. However, this mindset can lead to avoidable mistakes. Take the time to carefully read each question, consider each of the four options, and apply your knowledge before resorting to guesswork. Maintaining focus and discipline is key to maximizing the benefits of the four-choice format without sacrificing accuracy.

The shift to four answer choices in the Math section provides several strategic advantages, from improved guessing odds to reduced cognitive load. However, to fully capitalize on these changes, students must practice their elimination techniques, remain disciplined, and strengthen their math fundamentals. By doing so, you can approach the test with greater confidence and make the most of the opportunities this new format provides.

Guessing strategies and when to use them

In a timed and high-stakes exam, guessing can become an essential part of your test-taking strategy. While preparation and knowledge are your main tools for success, there will inevitably be questions that challenge you or take more time than you're willing to invest. Knowing when and how to guess strategically can make a significant difference in your final score. With the 2025 changes to the exam format, including the optional Science and Writing sections, this approach becomes even more relevant.

When to Guess

The key to effective guessing is knowing when it's your best option. Ideally, you should guess when:

1. Time is running out: If you're close to the end of a section and haven't finished answering all the questions, it's better to guess than to leave questions blank. Even a random guess gives you a 25% chance of getting the answer right, whereas an unanswered question has a 0% chance.

2. You're unsure after narrowing down options: Often, you can eliminate one or two clearly incorrect answers, even if you're not sure of the correct one. This increases your odds of guessing correctly, making it a more effective strategy than random guessing. For example, narrowing down four options to two gives you a 50% chance of guessing correctly—significantly better than random selection.

3. The question involves complex calculations or reasoning you don't have time for: In sections like Math or Science, if you know the question will take too much time or involves multiple steps, guessing may be a better option, particularly if you've identified some key information that allows you to eliminate incorrect answers.

How to Guess Strategically

When guessing, the aim is to use whatever information is available to increase your odds of choosing the correct answer. Here are some strategies to keep in mind:

1. Eliminate obvious wrong answers: The first step in any guessing strategy is to identify options that are clearly incorrect. For instance, in Math problems, certain answer choices might be obviously out of range, or in Science, a conclusion might not align with the data presented. The more answers you can eliminate, the better your chances of guessing the correct one.

2. Look for patterns in answer choices: In some cases, answer patterns can provide clues. For example, if two of the four choices are very similar, it might indicate that one of them is correct. Conversely, if one answer is significantly different in style, length, or detail, it could either be a distractor or the correct answer. Be careful not to rely on this too heavily, but it's worth considering when you're stuck.

3. Prioritize certain answer choices: If you have no idea and are guessing completely at random, research suggests that it's often statistically advantageous to guess the same letter consistently when forced to do so. While this may sound simple, it prevents you from wasting time second-guessing yourself on completely unknown answers.

Guessing in the Science and Writing Sections

In the optional Science section, guessing becomes particularly important if you're running out of time. Many Science questions require you to interpret data from charts, graphs, or tables. If you can quickly glean some key information (e.g., the trend in a graph or a key data point in a table), you might be able to eliminate one or two answers. The remaining options may still require a guess, but it's an educated one rather than a blind choice.

In the Writing section, if you're tasked with making decisions about essay structure, clarity, or tone, guessing works differently. Writing questions tend to have subtler differences between answer choices. The best approach here is to apply general rules—such as preferring clear and concise language over more complex or wordy alternatives—and eliminate answers that seem overly complicated or verbose. Guessing within these parameters increases your odds of choosing the best option.

Mental Approach to Guessing

It's important to stay calm while guessing. The mental pressure of time can cause students to panic, leading to rushed decisions and hasty guesses. Practice remaining composed in these moments and remember that guessing doesn't mean you've failed to answer the question correctly. It's part of a broader strategy aimed at maximizing your score by answering as many questions as possible, even if some of them require educated guesses.

Practice for Confidence

Effective guessing is a skill that can be practiced. During your study sessions, get used to narrowing down answer choices and making educated guesses. This will build confidence in your ability to quickly assess questions, eliminate wrong answers, and make more informed choices when you have to guess under pressure.

Guessing strategically is not about taking wild chances—it's about maximizing your odds when you're unsure and managing your time wisely. By incorporating these strategies into your test preparation, you can approach each section with confidence, knowing that even if you don't know every answer, you've got a plan to handle the tougher questions efficiently.

Avoiding common pitfalls

When it comes to excelling on a timed test, two of the most common pitfalls are misreading the question and running out of time. Both can drastically affect your score, no matter how well-prepared you are in terms of content knowledge. Understanding how to avoid these mistakes is essential for navigating the test efficiently and maximizing your performance. With a strategic approach, you can minimize these errors and ensure that you handle each section of the test with clarity and focus.

Misreading the Question

Misreading the question is a frequent mistake, often made under the pressure of time. It's easy to rush through the instructions, assuming you know what the question is asking, only to discover later that a small detail was overlooked. This can lead to incorrect answers, even if you understand the subject matter. Misreading can happen in any section, whether it's a subtle wording issue in an English question or misunderstanding a graph in the Science section.

To avoid misreading questions, slow down and carefully read the entire prompt before attempting to answer. One common tactic is to underline or highlight key terms in the question. For example, words like "except," "not," or "only" are often crucial to understanding what the question is truly asking, but they can be easily overlooked. By highlighting these words, you ensure that your focus is on the precise task required. For instance, if a question asks, "Which of the following is not true?" and you miss the word "not," you'll likely end up choosing the wrong answer, even if your understanding of the topic is accurate.

Additionally, in sections like Math, it's important to recheck the wording of the question, especially if it asks for specific units (e.g., feet instead of inches) or specific calculations (e.g., perimeter vs. area). Ensure that your final answer matches exactly what the question is asking. A common mistake occurs when students solve for one variable but forget that the question is asking for a different one, such as the value of a related angle or the result in a different measurement system.

Running Out of Time

The second major pitfall is running out of time. This can occur when you spend too long on difficult questions or when you mismanage your pacing throughout the test. In timed exams, every second counts, and balancing speed with accuracy is a skill that needs to be developed through practice.

One of the best strategies to avoid running out of time is to pace yourself from the start. Before you begin a section, take a moment to quickly skim through the questions and note any that look particularly challenging. These are the questions you can skip initially and return to later if time permits. By focusing on the easier questions first, you ensure that you accumulate as many points as possible before tackling the harder ones. This strategy is often referred to as "triage," where you handle the most manageable tasks first.

Additionally, practicing with a timer is essential. Familiarity with timed conditions helps build the instinct to know when to move on from a question. If you spend more than a minute struggling with a problem, it's usually better to make an educated guess and continue. This way, you ensure that you at least attempt every question rather than leaving any unanswered due to time constraints.

Another important tactic is to regularly check the clock. Divide the time you have for each section by the number of questions, and periodically assess whether you're staying on track. If you notice that you're falling behind, adjust your pace accordingly to avoid a last-minute rush.

Both misreading questions and running out of time are common mistakes that can have a big impact on your performance. To avoid them, take the time to carefully read and understand each question before jumping to conclusions, and practice effective time management to ensure that you can answer every question to the best of your ability. With discipline, practice, and attention to detail, these pitfalls can be minimized, allowing you to focus on showcasing your knowledge and skills.

The importance of mock tests

Mock tests are one of the most powerful tools in preparing for standardized exams, providing a realistic way to simulate the actual testing environment. Their importance cannot be overstated when it comes to refining your test-taking strategies, identifying weak spots, and building both confidence and endurance. Effective use of mock tests can turn a solid study plan into a successful one by transforming theoretical knowledge into practical application.

The first reason mock tests are so crucial is that they help you become familiar with the test format. No matter how well you know the material, it's easy to feel overwhelmed on test day if you're not comfortable with the test's structure. A mock test replicates the conditions you'll experience in the real exam—same sections, time constraints, and question types—allowing you to get used to the pacing and rhythm of the exam. The more familiar you are with the format, the less likely you'll feel anxious when it counts. This can be particularly helpful for students who struggle with the pressure of timed tests.

Additionally, mock tests are invaluable for identifying weaknesses. When you review your results afterward, patterns will emerge that show which topics or types of questions are causing the most difficulty. This insight helps you adjust your study plan to focus on areas where you need improvement. For example, you may find that you're struggling with specific math concepts or that reading comprehension questions take you longer than they should. By honing in on these areas, you can make your study time much more efficient, rather than spending equal time on topics where you're already strong.

Time management is another skill that mock tests help develop. One of the biggest challenges in any timed exam is striking the right balance between speed and accuracy. Mock tests allow you to practice pacing under realistic conditions. After completing several practice tests, you'll start to get a feel for how long to spend on each question and when it's time to move on. For example, you might notice that you're spending too much time on more difficult questions, leaving little time for easier ones. Once you identify this habit, you can work on quickly answering questions you know and returning to more difficult ones later.

Equally important is that mock tests help build endurance. Sitting for a multi-hour exam can be mentally exhausting, especially when you're focused and trying to perform at your best. By regularly completing full-length mock tests, you train your brain and body to sustain concentration over long periods. This helps reduce mental fatigue on the actual test day, ensuring that you maintain focus and accuracy even in the final stretch of the exam.

Moreover, mock tests are a great tool for practicing test-day strategies, such as guessing and skipping questions you don't immediately know how to answer. With each mock test, you refine these tactics, improving your overall score by making better decisions under time pressure. If you practice guessing wisely—by eliminating obvious wrong answers—you increase your chances of earning points on questions where you may not be fully confident.

Finally, it's important to review your mock test results carefully. Simply completing practice exams without reflecting on your performance won't lead to improvement. Go through each question you missed, understanding why the correct answer was right and why your answer was wrong. This reflection helps reinforce the concepts you missed and prevents you from making the same mistakes again.

Mock tests are an indispensable part of your preparation strategy. They provide a realistic experience, highlight areas for improvement, help manage time and stress, and build the endurance needed to succeed. The more you practice under test-like conditions, the better equipped you will be to perform when it counts.

Chapter 3: English Section: Grammar, Style, and Efficiency

Focus on shorter passages

In the English section, one of the most important skills to develop is efficiently managing the shorter passages and completing 50 questions within the allotted 35 minutes. This section tests your ability to understand and apply grammar rules, improve sentence structure, and make rhetorical decisions, all while maintaining a quick and steady pace. The challenge is balancing speed and accuracy, as misreading or overanalyzing can cost you precious time.

The first step in handling these shorter passages effectively is to recognize their length as an advantage. Unlike longer, more complex reading sections, these passages allow you to quickly engage with the material and focus more on the technical aspects of grammar, punctuation, and sentence structure. These are elements that can often be approached systematically once you are familiar with the core rules.

When approaching the questions, a systematic approach to grammar is essential. For example, many questions will focus on sentence structure, subject-verb agreement, punctuation, and word choice. It's crucial to develop a strong foundation in these areas so you can quickly spot errors. For instance, knowing common punctuation rules like when to use commas, semicolons, or colons can save you time. Familiarity with these rules allows you to answer certain questions almost instinctively without needing to analyze the entire passage in depth. These quick wins on straightforward grammar questions give you more time for the more complex rhetorical or style-related ones.

Another important tactic for efficiency is to look at the questions before reading the passage. This technique helps you know what to focus on while reading. Since each question is directly related to a specific part of the passage, you don't need to read every word as you would for a literature analysis. Instead, you can scan the passage for the information needed to answer the questions, whether they're testing punctuation, sentence placement, or overall structure.

Additionally, focus on rhetorical skills questions that test your ability to improve clarity and conciseness. These questions ask you to decide if certain sentences should be revised or omitted, or if a specific transition sentence improves the passage. When dealing with rhetorical questions, always keep in mind that clarity and simplicity are often the best choices. Long-winded, overly complex sentences are rarely the correct answer, as the goal is typically to make the passage clearer and more concise. Avoid the temptation to overthink these questions; trust that the shortest, clearest option is usually the best choice.

Efficiency is also about skipping the tough questions and returning to them later. If a certain question or set of answer choices feels difficult or time-consuming, it's better to move on and answer the easier questions first. This keeps your momentum going and ensures you're not wasting valuable minutes on a single difficult question. You can always return to those questions at the end if time allows.

Lastly, practice plays a critical role in improving both speed and accuracy. The more you expose yourself to practice passages and timed drills, the more you'll develop an intuitive sense for what to look for in each type of question. Familiarity with the format and content builds confidence, and with time, you'll naturally become quicker at identifying errors and making decisions.

Key grammar rules tested on the ACT

The English section of standardized tests consistently examines students' understanding and application of core grammar rules. Mastering these rules is essential for efficiently answering grammar-based questions. These questions are designed to test your ability to identify errors in sentence structure, punctuation, and word usage, all of which contribute to clear and concise writing. Below, we explore the key grammar rules you'll encounter, along with strategies to recognize and apply them.

1. Subject-Verb Agreement

One of the most fundamental grammar rules tested involves ensuring that the subject and verb in a sentence agree in number. This means that a singular subject must be paired with a singular verb, while a plural subject requires a plural verb. For example:

- Correct: The dog runs through the park. (singular subject and verb)

- Incorrect: The dog run through the park. In many cases, prepositional phrases or clauses between the subject and the verb can make it harder to see this relationship, so it's essential to isolate the subject and verb when reviewing these types of questions.

2. Pronoun-Antecedent Agreement

Another common area tested is the agreement between a pronoun and its antecedent (the noun to which it refers). Pronouns must agree in number and gender with the antecedent. For instance:

- Correct: Each student brought his book. (singular pronoun for singular antecedent)

- Incorrect: Each student brought their book. Pronouns should also be clear about which noun they are replacing. If the pronoun's antecedent is ambiguous, the sentence becomes unclear and needs to be revised.

3. Punctuation: Commas, Semicolons and Colons

Punctuation questions often test your ability to use commas, semicolons, and colons correctly.

- Commas: These are used to separate elements in a list, after introductory phrases, or between independent clauses when connected by a conjunction (e.g., and, but, or). Overusing or misplacing commas can lead to comma splices or disrupt sentence flow.

- Semicolons: Used to separate two closely related independent clauses without a conjunction. For example: I went to the store; I bought some bread.

- Colons: Typically used before a list or explanation. For instance: She brought three things: a notebook, a pen, and her textbook.

4. Modifiers: Placement and Clarity

Modifiers, whether they are words or phrases, must be placed near the word they modify to ensure clarity. Misplaced or dangling modifiers can confuse the reader about who or what is performing the action. Consider the following:

- Correct: Running down the street, the dog chased the ball.

- Incorrect: Running down the street, the ball was chased by the dog. In the incorrect sentence, it sounds like the ball is running down the street, which makes no sense.

5. Parallel Structure

Parallelism involves ensuring that elements in a sentence that are similar in function are also similar in form. This is often tested in lists or comparisons. For example:

- Correct: She likes reading, writing, and swimming.

- Incorrect: She likes reading, writing, and to swim. In the incorrect sentence, "to swim" breaks the parallel structure established by the gerunds "reading" and "writing."

6. Verb Tense Consistency

Maintaining consistent verb tenses within a sentence or paragraph is crucial for clear communication. If the sentence shifts between tenses without reason, it becomes confusing. For example:

- Correct: He was walking to the store when he realized he had forgotten his wallet.

- Incorrect: He was walking to the store when he realizes he had forgotten his wallet.

7. Idiomatic Expressions and Word Choice

Standardized tests often include questions that require you to choose the correct idiomatic expression or ensure the proper use of commonly confused words (e.g., affect vs. effect, their vs. there vs. they're). Idiomatic expressions are fixed phrases where a specific preposition is required:

- Correct: She is interested in science.
- Incorrect: She is interested on science.

Mastering these grammar rules is essential for success in the English section. The more familiar you are with these rules, the quicker you'll be able to identify errors and select the correct answer. Regular practice with sentence corrections and grammar drills will solidify these concepts and help you develop an intuitive sense for clear, grammatically correct writing.

Sentence structure, rhetorical skills and style

Understanding sentence structure, rhetorical skills, and writing style is essential to mastering the English section of any standardized exam. This section evaluates not just your grasp of grammar, but also your ability to recognize and improve the clarity, conciseness, and effectiveness of writing. Mastering these elements can help you move beyond identifying grammatical errors and into shaping writing that communicates more effectively.

Sentence Structure

At the core of strong writing is effective sentence structure, which includes how clauses, phrases, and punctuation are used to convey meaning. Sentence structure can vary from simple to complex, and recognizing the purpose of each helps you determine whether it is effective or needs revision.

- Simple Sentences: These contain just one independent clause and convey a straightforward idea. For instance, "The dog barked." While simple sentences can be effective for clarity, too many of them can make writing feel choppy.

- Compound Sentences: These join two or more independent clauses with conjunctions (e.g., and, but, or). They're useful for combining related ideas: "The dog barked, and the cat ran away." However, ensure that the ideas linked by compound sentences are logically connected.

- Complex Sentences: These include an independent clause and one or more dependent clauses, which add detail or context: "When the dog barked, the cat ran away." This type of structure allows for more nuance but can be misused if the dependent clause makes the sentence confusing.

Good sentence structure often balances simplicity and complexity, allowing for variety without overcomplicating the ideas presented. Identifying run-on sentences, sentence fragments, or sentences that lack clarity due to convoluted structure is key to improving writing.

Rhetorical Skills

Beyond sentence mechanics, strong writing involves rhetorical skills, which address how ideas are presented and organized. This includes the overall flow of a passage and the impact of specific word choices, sentence order, and paragraph structure.

- Purpose and Audience: One of the first rhetorical considerations is the purpose of the text. Is it designed to inform, persuade, or entertain? Knowing the intent behind the passage informs decisions about tone and word choice. For example, a persuasive passage might employ stronger, more assertive language, while an informative text favors clarity and precision.

- Clarity and Conciseness: Often, questions will ask you to choose between more concise and verbose sentences. In most cases, the best choice will be the one that communicates the idea clearly with fewer words. Eliminating unnecessary words or repetitive phrases is a fundamental part of revising for conciseness. Consider this example: "Due to the fact that he was late, we missed the meeting." can be simplified to, "Because he was late, we missed the meeting."

- Transitions and Flow: Effective writing doesn't just present ideas; it connects them smoothly. Pay attention to transitions between sentences and paragraphs. Phrases like "however," "therefore," or "in contrast" can guide the reader through shifts in argument or perspective. Poor transitions can leave the reader disoriented, while strong ones lead to better comprehension.

Style

Style encompasses how the writer's choices in diction, tone, and sentence structure contribute to the overall feel of the passage. Mastering style means recognizing when writing feels too casual, too formal, or when it veers off into ambiguity.

- Tone and Voice: Different passages require different tones—whether formal, conversational, or somewhere in between. Recognizing shifts in tone and identifying when a sentence doesn't match the overall voice of the passage is crucial. For example, formal writing would avoid slang or overly casual phrases, whereas a narrative or creative passage might use more conversational language for authenticity.

- Word Choice: Effective word choice focuses on precision and avoiding ambiguity. For instance, words that are too general or vague can weaken an argument. Choosing a more specific or descriptive term often makes the writing stronger. Likewise, overly technical jargon can confuse readers, so it's important to choose words that match the level of understanding the audience has.

Mastering sentence structure, rhetorical skills, and style involves more than just spotting grammatical errors—it's about improving the effectiveness and clarity of communication. By focusing on how sentences are constructed, how ideas are organized, and how tone and word choice influence a passage's message, you can become adept at not just answering questions correctly but improving writing in a meaningful way. Practice in these areas will not only help you in tests but in any form of written communication.

Practice drills: 10-minute challenges to maximize efficiency

Practice drills are one of the most effective ways to build efficiency and accuracy when preparing for the English section of standardized exams. The key is to focus on time management and the ability to quickly recognize and apply grammar rules, sentence structure, and rhetorical skills under timed conditions. One highly effective technique is the use of 10-minute challenges, where you focus on completing a specific set of tasks within a short, fixed period. These drills help condition your brain to work under pressure, much like the conditions you'll face during the actual test.

The Purpose of 10-Minute Challenges

The primary purpose of 10-minute challenges is to simulate the real exam environment in a controlled, focused way. With only 10 minutes on the clock, these exercises force you to manage your time efficiently, make quick decisions, and avoid overthinking questions. This is crucial for a timed exam where hesitation and overanalysis can lead to lost points. These short bursts of practice build endurance, speed, and mental sharpness.

Designing Effective 10-Minute Drills

To get the most out of your practice, each 10-minute drill should target specific areas that will help you sharpen both your grammar skills and your ability to quickly analyze passages for errors in sentence structure and rhetorical style.

- Grammar Rule Drill: One of the easiest drills to begin with is focused solely on grammar rules. In this drill, choose 10 questions that cover a variety of grammar topics—subject-verb agreement, pronoun usage, punctuation, and verb tense consistency. The goal is to see how quickly you can identify errors and correct them, but with accuracy as your top priority. By setting a 10-minute time limit, you'll learn to spot common grammar mistakes more efficiently, which is critical for success on the test.

- Sentence Structure Drill: Another drill could focus on identifying and improving sentence structure. In this 10-minute period, choose a set of questions that ask you to correct sentence fragments, run-on sentences, or misplaced modifiers. This helps you develop an eye for structural issues that might make a sentence unclear or grammatically incorrect. As you practice, you'll find that you can recognize these problems faster, allowing you to move through these types of questions more efficiently during the real exam.

- Conciseness and Style Drill: A drill centered around rhetorical skills—such as improving clarity and conciseness—can help you enhance your ability to choose the most effective revisions in a passage. In 10 minutes, go through several questions where you need to eliminate wordiness or improve the flow of the writing. By the end of the drill, you should feel more confident in making concise and clear choices under time constraints.

Increasing Difficulty Over Time

As you become more comfortable with the 10-minute challenges, increase the difficulty of the drills to ensure continuous improvement. Start by selecting easier questions, then gradually incorporate more complex or nuanced questions that require deeper reasoning or more advanced grammatical knowledge. This not only ensures that you're improving but also helps you maintain a steady pace throughout various levels of difficulty.

Additionally, it's important to vary the types of questions within a single drill. This is because on test day, questions are often mixed, requiring you to switch quickly between grammar rules, sentence structure revisions, and rhetorical analysis. Mixing question types in your 10-minute challenges mimics this experience, helping you build flexibility in your thinking and response.

Tracking Progress and Identifying Weaknesses

After each 10-minute drill, review your answers carefully. This is just as important as the timed practice itself. Take note of which questions took you the longest and which types of errors you missed most often. By doing this, you can adjust your study plan to focus on the areas where you need the most improvement. Over time, you'll notice patterns in your mistakes, allowing you to target your weaknesses more effectively.

The Role of Consistency

Consistency is key to mastering these challenges. Doing just one or two drills won't have the same impact as committing to several short bursts of practice over the course of a week. Set aside regular time each day to complete at least one 10-minute drill. These brief, focused practice sessions will add up, resulting in better time management and a stronger grasp of the rules and concepts you'll encounter on test day.

In summary, 10-minute practice drills are an excellent way to build speed, efficiency, and confidence for the English section. By targeting specific areas, increasing difficulty over time, and consistently reviewing your progress, you'll ensure that you're not only practicing effectively but also improving steadily in the areas that matter most.

Chapter 4: Math Section: Concepts, Speed, and Calculations

The 50-minute breakdown for 45 Math questions

The math section of standardized tests is one of the most challenging parts for many students, and the updated format, which allocates 50 minutes for 45 math questions, adds a new layer of complexity. While the extra time per question can seem beneficial, the tradeoff is that the questions tend to be more challenging and demand more critical thinking and problem-solving skills. Understanding how to manage your time effectively and approach these harder questions strategically is essential for success.

More Time Per Question

With 50 minutes to complete 45 questions, students have a bit more than a minute per question, which is an improvement over the previous format. However, this extra time should not lead to complacency. Instead, it's important to treat the additional time as an opportunity to work through complex questions carefully rather than rush.

For example, certain algebraic or geometry problems that require multiple steps to solve can now be tackled with a clearer mind, knowing you have slightly more time. This allows for checking your work on more involved questions, especially those where a misstep could lead to an incorrect answer. Despite the additional time, it's still important to practice solving questions efficiently and know when to move on if a question is taking too long.

Harder Questions Demand More Thought

While the extra time is a benefit, the difficulty of the questions has increased in this revised format. You'll encounter questions that require a deeper understanding of mathematical concepts and the application of those concepts in non-obvious ways. Many questions will involve several layers of problem-solving, such as integrating algebra with geometry or understanding how different mathematical principles connect in one problem.

Take, for example, a geometry problem that not only asks for the area of a triangle but also incorporates knowledge of the Pythagorean theorem or trigonometric identities. In these cases, it's essential to know which formulas apply and how to connect different pieces of information within the problem. This complexity makes it crucial for students to be comfortable with a wide range of math concepts, from basic arithmetic to more advanced topics like trigonometry and probability.

Prioritizing Questions: Easy vs. Hard

To manage the difficulty effectively, it's important to prioritize questions as you work through the section. Begin by identifying the questions that fall within your area of strength or those that appear straightforward. Answering these easier questions first ensures that you rack up points quickly and build confidence early in the test.

As you move through the test, mark harder or time-consuming questions that you can return to later. By doing so, you ensure that you don't waste too much time on a single difficult problem at the expense of other questions you could answer correctly. This strategy helps you avoid the common pitfall of getting stuck on one challenging question and running out of time before finishing the section.

Breaking Down Multi-Step Problems

Many of the harder questions in the new math format are multi-step problems that require careful breakdown. For instance, you might encounter a problem that requires you to first solve for one variable before using that value to solve for another unknown in a different equation. These types of questions often require more time to think through, but they are manageable if you stay calm and methodical.

Approach these problems by breaking them into smaller, more manageable tasks. Focus on solving the first step, and don't let the complexity of the entire question overwhelm you. By taking it one step at a time, you're more likely to reach the correct answer without becoming frustrated or making careless mistakes.

Maximizing Efficiency During Practice

To perform well in the math section, it's important to practice regularly and under timed conditions. While practicing, time yourself as if you're in the real exam setting to get a feel for how long each type of question takes. The more you practice under these conditions, the more natural and efficient you will become at answering questions within the given time frame.

Practice also allows you to become familiar with common question types and formats, reducing the time needed to understand what the question is asking. The quicker you can identify what kind of math problem you're dealing with—whether it's algebraic, geometric, or trigonometric—the faster you can get to work on solving it.

The updated math section's allocation of 50 minutes for 45 questions offers more time per question, but the increased difficulty means that students need to manage their time wisely and approach questions with a strong strategic mindset. By practicing regularly, focusing on understanding key mathematical concepts, and developing effective problem-solving techniques, students can maximize their performance in this section and tackle even the hardest questions with confidence.

Core topics: Algebra, geometry, statistics and trigonometry

In the math section, questions focus on four core topics: algebra, geometry, statistics, and trigonometry. Mastering these subjects is essential for performing well on this part of the test, as they form the foundation of the questions. Let's explore each topic in detail, providing an overview of the key concepts and strategies necessary for tackling these questions effectively.

Algebra

Algebra is a central part of the math section, covering a range of topics such as equations, inequalities, functions, and linear relationships. The questions typically require you to solve for unknowns, manipulate expressions, and understand the relationships between variables.

Key areas to focus on:

- **Linear equations and inequalities**: You'll encounter questions asking you to solve for a variable or determine the solution set for inequalities.
- **Quadratic equations**: Recognizing quadratic forms and applying the quadratic formula is crucial.
- **Functions and their graphs**: Understanding how to read and interpret function graphs, as well as identifying domain and range, is a common requirement.
- **Polynomials**: Factoring and expanding polynomials, as well as solving polynomial equations, is another critical area.

An effective approach to algebra questions is to practice simplifying equations, using substitution, and breaking down complex expressions into manageable parts. Consistency in practicing algebraic manipulations will help improve speed and accuracy.

Geometry

Geometry questions make up a significant portion of the math section. These questions test your understanding of shapes, sizes, and the properties of space. Many of the problems involve calculating areas, perimeters, volumes, and using geometric theorems to solve for unknown values.

Key areas to focus on:

- **Triangles**: You must be familiar with the properties of various types of triangles, including right triangles, and apply the Pythagorean theorem.
- **Circles**: Calculating the circumference, area, and understanding the relationships between angles, chords, and tangents are frequently tested.
- **Polygons and quadrilaterals**: Expect questions about the properties of different polygons, especially rectangles, squares, parallelograms, and trapezoids.

- **Coordinate geometry**: This area includes plotting points on the coordinate plane, calculating distances between points, and finding the equations of lines.

In geometry, it's helpful to visualize the problem by drawing diagrams when one isn't provided. This allows you to identify relationships between shapes and apply the correct formulas efficiently.

Statistics

Statistics questions focus on interpreting data, understanding probability, and analyzing various statistical measures. These problems often involve interpreting charts, graphs, or tables and calculating statistical values like mean, median, and mode.

Key areas to focus on:

- **Probability**: You might be asked to calculate the probability of simple and compound events, or use probability rules to solve more complex problems.
- **Mean, median, mode**: Understanding how to calculate and interpret these measures of central tendency is crucial.
- **Data interpretation**: Being able to read graphs, tables, and charts, as well as making sense of data trends, is frequently tested.

For statistics, practice working with different data sets and calculating probabilities quickly. The ability to interpret visual data efficiently can help you gain extra time for more difficult problems.

Trigonometry

Trigonometry, though less emphasized compared to algebra and geometry, is still a crucial part of the math section. The questions typically require knowledge of trigonometric ratios and their applications in solving problems related to angles and sides of triangles.

Key areas to focus on:

- **Trigonometric ratios**: Be comfortable using sine, cosine, and tangent functions to solve for unknown sides or angles in right triangles.
- **Unit circle and radian measure**: Understanding the unit circle and converting between degrees and radians is useful for certain types of questions.
- **Trigonometric identities**: You may also need to apply basic identities like the Pythagorean identity to solve equations involving trigonometric functions.

For trigonometry, focus on practicing problems involving right triangles and trigonometric ratios, and ensure you can use your calculator efficiently for more complex angle measures.

Mastering these four core topics (algebra, geometry, statistics and trigonometry) will provide a strong foundation for success in the math section. Each topic requires a mix of conceptual understanding and practical problem-solving skills. By consistently practicing a variety of problems within these categories, you will develop the speed, accuracy, and confidence necessary to perform well. Keep in mind that understanding when and how to apply formulas and strategies efficiently is key to navigating through the section smoothly.

Essential formulas and calculator tips

In the math section, understanding essential formulas and how to use your calculator *efficiently* is critical to success. While the math test covers a wide range of topics, many questions rely on the correct application of basic formulas and calculations that you need to have ready at your fingertips. Additionally, mastering calculator strategies can help you solve complex problems quickly and accurately. Let's dive into the most important formulas you'll need to know, followed by some valuable calculator tips to optimize your performance.

Essential Formulas

Familiarity with essential math formulas allows you to solve problems efficiently without having to derive them from scratch during the test. Here are some of the most important formulas you'll need:

1. Algebraic Formulas

Slope of a Line: slope $= \dfrac{y_2 - y_1}{x_2 - x_1}$

Quadratic Formula: $x = \dfrac{-b \pm \sqrt{b^2 - 4ac}}{2a}$

Equation of a Line: $y = mx + b$ where m is the slope and b is the y-intercept.

Distance Formula: $d = \sqrt{(x_2 - x_1)^2 + (y_2 - y_1)^2}$

These algebraic formulas are commonly used to solve questions related to graphs, slopes, and distances between points.

2. Geometry Formulas

Area of a Circle: $A = \pi r^2$

Circumference of a Circle: $C = 2\pi r$

Area of a Triangle: $A = \dfrac{1}{2} \ base \ x \ height$

Pythagorean Theorem: $a^2 + b^2 = c^2$ (for right triangles)

Volume of a Cylinder: $V = \pi r^2 h$

Knowing these basic geometry formulas helps solve questions that ask for areas, volumes, and perimeters. Geometry problems often present diagrams, so recognizing when to apply these formulas is crucial.

3. Trigonometry Formulas

Sine, Cosine, Tangent: $\sin\emptyset = \dfrac{opposite}{hypotenuse}$, $\cos\emptyset = \dfrac{adjacent}{hypotenuse}$, $\tan \emptyset = \dfrac{opposit}{adjacent}$

SOH-CAH-TOA: This mnemonic helps remember the relationships between sides in right-angle triangles.

These trigonometric ratios are fundamental in solving problems that involve angles and distances in triangles.

4.Statistics Formulas

Mean (Average): mean $= \dfrac{sum\ of\ all\ values}{number\ of\ values}$

Probability: $P(event) = \dfrac{number\ of\ favorable\ outcomes}{total\ number\ of\ outcomes}$

In problems related to data interpretation and probability, these formulas help you navigate through calculations efficiently.

Calculator Tips

1. While you're not expected to memorize overly complex formulas, using a calculator effectively can save time and ensure accuracy in the math section. Here are some key calculator strategies:

2. Master Your Calculator's Functions Make sure you're familiar with the various functions your calculator offers, such as square roots, exponents, and trigonometric functions. For instance, knowing how to quickly switch between degrees and radians for trigonometric calculations can be a time-saver. Additionally, using the fraction-to-decimal conversion feature allows you to simplify complex fractions quickly.

3. Use Parentheses to Avoid Errors When entering longer or more complicated calculations, always use parentheses to keep operations in the correct order. For example, if you're calculating (3+5)×2, entering it without parentheses could lead to mistakes if you're rushing. Parentheses help the calculator prioritize operations correctly.

4. Estimate First, Calculate Second For many questions, it's useful to estimate an answer before using your calculator. Estimation can help you determine whether the calculator's result is reasonable, especially in cases where you might have mistyped a value or hit the wrong button. Quick mental math can help cross-check your final answer.

5. Use the Memory Function Many calculators have a memory function (often labeled as "M+" or "MR") that allows you to store intermediate results. This can be useful when solving multi-step problems, as it allows you to avoid re-entering the same numbers multiple times. It's especially helpful in questions where you need to reuse the same value for different calculations.

6. Know When Not to Use the Calculator Although the calculator is a great tool, some questions can be solved more quickly without it. Basic arithmetic, recognizing simple multiples, or applying simple geometric formulas can sometimes be faster than keying everything into the calculator. The key is knowing when to rely on mental math or paper-and-pencil methods instead of the calculator.

Success in the math section requires a balance between understanding essential formulas and using your calculator effectively. By mastering the core formulas for algebra, geometry, trigonometry, and statistics, you'll be able to approach a wide range of problems confidently. Combined with strategic calculator use—such as knowing its functions, using parentheses to ensure accuracy, and estimating before calculating—you'll maximize your efficiency and accuracy. Consistent practice with both formulas and calculator techniques will ensure you're prepared for even the most challenging math questions.

Practice techniques for speed: Answering confidently within time limits

Mastering the math section requires both a solid understanding of the material and the ability to answer questions within strict time constraints. Success hinges not only on your grasp of the concepts but also on how effectively you can apply those concepts under pressure. Developing practice techniques for speed is essential to answering confidently within the time limits. These techniques, when regularly implemented, help improve accuracy, minimize mistakes, and ensure that you complete the section within the allocated time.

Building a Strong Foundation with Timed Practice

Before focusing on speed, it's crucial to build a strong foundation by mastering the concepts and formulas commonly tested. Start by practicing questions without time constraints to ensure you fully understand the material. Once you have a firm grasp, introduce timing into your practice sessions.

Timed practice is key to improving speed. Set a timer for small sets of questions (e.g., 10 to 15 questions) and gradually decrease the time as you improve. For example, begin by giving yourself two minutes per question and gradually reduce that to one minute. This helps condition your mind to work under pressure while maintaining accuracy.

Prioritization: Know When to Skip and Return

Not all questions are created equal, and some will take more time to solve than others. Prioritizing questions based on their difficulty level is a crucial speed technique. Start with the questions you can solve quickly and confidently. These "low-hanging fruit" questions help you accumulate points early in the section, leaving more time for the challenging ones.

If a question seems too difficult or time-consuming, don't hesitate to skip it and return later. Spending too much time on a single problem can prevent you from answering easier questions that could boost your score. Mark the skipped questions, and revisit them once you've completed the rest of the section.

Chunking Problems: Break Down Multi-Step Questions

Some math problems require multiple steps to solve, and these can be particularly time-consuming. Chunking is a technique that involves breaking these complex problems into smaller, more manageable steps. By solving each step one at a time, you avoid feeling overwhelmed and reduce the chances of making mistakes. This approach also speeds up the problem-solving process because it allows you to stay focused on one aspect of the problem at a time.

Develop Quick Recognition Patterns

Over time, you'll notice that many test questions follow similar formats or patterns. Pattern recognition can significantly reduce the time it takes to solve certain types of problems. For example, algebraic equations often require similar steps, such as isolating variables or factoring, while geometry problems frequently involve common formulas for areas or angles.

Practicing regularly with a wide variety of problem types helps you develop an intuition for which strategies to apply to each question type. The quicker you can identify the underlying pattern, the faster you can solve the problem.

Use Estimation and Elimination

Another technique for saving time involves using estimation and elimination. For questions that require lengthy calculations, try estimating the answer first. Often, this allows you to eliminate one or two answer choices right away. If the question involves large or complex numbers, rounding can help you get a ballpark figure, making it easier to choose between the remaining options.

This technique is particularly useful in multiple-choice questions, where even if your estimate is slightly off, you can still arrive at the correct answer by eliminating the clearly wrong options.

Calculator Use: Speed and Accuracy

Using your calculator effectively is another key element in boosting speed. Familiarize yourself with all of your calculator's functions, including those for exponents, square roots, and trigonometric calculations. This will allow you to perform complex calculations quickly without getting bogged down in manual computations.

Additionally, avoid over-reliance on the calculator for simple calculations like addition, subtraction, or multiplication. Doing these basic calculations mentally or on paper can be faster than inputting them into the calculator, particularly for smaller numbers.

Regular Timed Mock Tests

Lastly, one of the best ways to build speed is by regularly taking timed mock tests. These full-length practice tests simulate the real exam environment, allowing you to gauge your speed and identify areas that require improvement. During mock tests, treat the timing as strictly as you would during the actual exam. This helps you build the endurance and focus needed to maintain a fast and steady pace throughout the test.

After each mock test, review the questions you got wrong or spent too much time on, and identify specific areas to improve. Over time, you'll develop an efficient rhythm and the confidence needed to handle time constraints.

Developing speed in the math section involves a combination of timed practice, strategic prioritization, and familiarity with common problem-solving patterns. By regularly applying these techniques—prioritizing easier questions, using chunking for multi-step problems, estimating answers, and optimizing calculator use—you'll be able to answer confidently within the time limits. Continuous practice and timed mock tests will further sharpen your skills, helping you achieve the balance between speed and accuracy needed for success.

Chapter 5: Reading Section: Comprehension and Interpretation

40 minutes for 36 questions

In the reading section, you are given 40 minutes to answer 36 questions across multiple shorter passages. Tackling these passages efficiently requires a combination of time management, reading comprehension strategies, and a sharp ability to interpret and analyze information quickly. To ensure that you finish within the time limit while answering accurately, a methodical approach is necessary.

The reading section is designed to present multiple shorter passages covering a range of topics, from fiction and literary analysis to scientific explanations and historical narratives. Each passage requires a slightly different approach depending on the subject matter, but they share common elements—each passage is packed with information in a condensed format. Therefore, it is essential to capture the main points as efficiently as possible.

Shorter passages may feel easier due to their length, but they can be just as complex as longer passages, often requiring closer attention to each sentence or paragraph. In many cases, a few lines of text might contain critical details needed to answer multiple questions. Thus, the ability to grasp meaning quickly and interpret the author's intent is key.

To manage your time effectively, you'll need to balance skimming and careful reading. Begin each passage by skimming the first few sentences, which will often provide an introduction or general idea of the content. This initial skim helps you grasp the main subject and the passage's tone. Next, review the questions briefly before diving into a more thorough reading. Having a sense of the questions will guide your focus as you go back to read the passage in detail.

After skimming, engage in careful reading of crucial parts of the passage. Focus on sections that introduce arguments, transitions in the author's line of thought, and any information directly related to the questions. Skimming allows you to save time by quickly identifying the overall structure, while careful reading helps in ensuring you correctly interpret the passage's essential details.

With 40 minutes to answer 36 questions, you have about 1 minute and 7 seconds per question, including the time required to read each passage. Therefore, time management is a critical skill for succeeding in this section. Allocate roughly 3-4 minutes for reading each passage, and reserve the remaining time for answering the associated questions.

A good strategy is to start with questions that involve direct information retrieval from the text. These questions are usually straightforward and can be answered more quickly than inference-based questions. This approach allows you to answer easier questions first, saving more time for the complex or interpretive ones later. Additionally, if a question seems time-consuming or confusing, skip it and return to it after completing the rest of the passage's questions. This ensures that you won't waste valuable time and will maximize the number of questions you can answer confidently.

Speed in the reading section improves through consistent practice with shorter passages and various text types. As you encounter more diverse reading materials, you'll become familiar with different writing styles and structures, which will help you process the information more rapidly. Focus on reading a range of texts, including literature, essays, scientific articles, and opinion pieces, as these will closely resemble the types of passages you'll face.

In your practice sessions, simulate real test conditions by timing yourself as you read and answer questions. Over time, you'll develop a rhythm that allows you to move fluidly from reading to answering questions without losing focus. Regular practice will also help you improve your ability to read critically while under time constraints.

Successfully navigating shorter passages in the reading section is all about finding the right balance between skimming for structure and reading for detail, while maintaining a clear strategy for managing time. By practicing these techniques, you can ensure that you stay within the time limit, capture the essential ideas of each passage, and confidently answer the questions posed. Consistency in your practice will help sharpen your reading skills and improve your overall performance.

Identifying key ideas and arguments quickly

Identifying key ideas and arguments quickly in the reading section is a critical skill for maximizing performance within the time limits. This ability allows you to focus on the most relevant parts of a passage and answer questions with confidence, all while managing your time effectively. By honing your skills in recognizing central points, arguments, and supporting details, you can navigate through the questions with more ease and accuracy.

The main idea of a passage refers to the overall message or point that the author is trying to convey. In shorter passages, this main idea is usually introduced within the first few sentences or paragraphs. Authors often start by framing a problem, posing a question, or providing background information that leads to their central thesis. To quickly identify this, you should focus on the introductory sentences, as they often provide a clear indication of what the passage will discuss.

In some cases, the main idea is reinforced through topic sentences at the beginning of each paragraph. These sentences help outline the key points that support the passage's overall argument. By paying attention to these topic sentences, you can quickly understand the structure of the passage and the flow of the argument without needing to read every detail.

While the main idea gives the overall framework, the supporting details and evidence provide the backbone of the argument. These details may include facts, examples, data, or quotes that reinforce the author's claim. To quickly locate these supporting points, it is helpful to identify keywords in the questions that guide you to specific parts of the passage.

When tackling passages that present an argument, notice the transitional phrases that signal the introduction of evidence or a shift in argument. Words like "for example," "because," or "in addition" often indicate that the author is providing evidence to back up their claims. By recognizing these markers, you can easily zoom in on the sections of the passage that contain the most important information.

While many questions may ask for explicit information directly from the passage, others require you to make inferences. Inference questions ask you to go beyond what is directly stated, requiring you to interpret the author's meaning or speculate about their intentions. To answer these questions effectively, you need to piece together the central argument and supporting details and consider what the author implies but doesn't state outright.

When identifying inferences, focus on tone and word choice, as these often reveal the author's attitude or suggest implications. For instance, an author might not explicitly criticize a viewpoint, but their word choices—like using "problematic" or "misguided"—can imply a negative stance.

It's important to understand that not every detail in a passage is essential. Secondary information, such as anecdotes, descriptive details, or background context, often supports the main idea but is not crucial to understanding the core argument. To save time, focus on identifying the key details that directly relate to the main point of the passage and the questions you are answering. These may include pivotal examples, statistical data, or direct statements that summarize the argument.

Avoid getting bogged down in overly detailed sections that don't contribute directly to the passage's argument. Practice distinguishing between key information and filler details to streamline your reading process.

The challenge in the reading section is balancing speed with accuracy. While it's essential to work quickly, it's equally important to ensure that your understanding of the passage is accurate. To develop this balance, practice reading a variety of texts—such as articles, essays, and reports—and summarizing their main points and arguments after a quick read-through. Over time, this will help you build the skill of identifying key ideas and arguments efficiently without sacrificing accuracy.

Additionally, work on scanning techniques that allow you to move quickly through passages without missing critical information. Scanning involves looking for key words, phrases, and ideas that directly relate to the main argument or central points of the text. This skill becomes especially useful when you need to return to specific parts of the passage to answer detailed questions.

Identifying key ideas and arguments quickly is an essential skill for success in the reading section. By focusing on main ideas, supporting details, and understanding when to infer meaning, you can improve your speed and accuracy. Practicing these techniques will allow you to work efficiently within the time constraints, ensuring you capture the most important points and arguments without getting lost in unnecessary details.

Practice drills for inference and analytical questions

Inference and analytical questions require a deeper level of reading comprehension because they ask you to go beyond what is explicitly stated in the text. These questions often test your ability to draw conclusions, interpret the author's intentions, and understand implications that are not directly expressed. To excel at these types of questions, it's crucial to develop specific skills through practice drills designed to improve both your inferencing abilities and analytical thinking. Below, we will explore some effective drills for improving your ability to tackle these questions confidently.

Inference Questions: Understanding Implications

Inference questions require you to deduce information that is not directly stated but is implied by the author. These questions often ask, "What can be inferred from the passage?" or "What does the author imply about this particular situation?"

To practice, start by reading short paragraphs or news articles where the author presents a point of view without explicitly stating their conclusion. After reading, ask yourself questions such as:

- What does the author assume the reader already knows?
- What is the author hinting at without saying it directly?
- Can I summarize the main idea without repeating the exact words?

You can use this drill to help you develop the habit of looking for subtext—the underlying message that isn't immediately obvious. Practice drawing logical conclusions based on subtle clues, such as tone, context, and word choice. With enough repetition, you'll become more adept at spotting these cues during the test.

Analytical Questions: Evaluating Arguments and Evidence

Analytical questions require a critical evaluation of the text, often asking you to assess the strength of the author's argument, the effectiveness of evidence presented, or the logical consistency of the passage. For example, you might be asked to identify assumptions, flaws in reasoning, or how well a conclusion follows from the evidence.

A good practice drill for analytical questions is to deconstruct argumentative essays or editorial pieces. Read these texts with a focus on:

- Identifying the central argument
- Listing the pieces of evidence, the author uses to support their claim
- Critically evaluating whether the evidence logically supports the argument

After analyzing the text, try to write down any counterarguments or logical fallacies you noticed. This exercise helps train your brain to critically evaluate the relationships between claims and evidence. It also encourages you to approach reading material with a more questioning attitude, which is essential for success with analytical questions.

Comparing Perspectives

Many analytical and inference-based questions require you to compare different viewpoints or recognize how various perspectives are presented. A useful drill involves reading opinion pieces that present conflicting views on the same subject. For this exercise:

- Read two articles or essays that discuss the same topic from different perspectives.
- Identify the core arguments in each and list the points where they agree or disagree.
- Analyze the evidence and tone each author uses to support their perspective.

This practice will not only help you improve your understanding of opposing viewpoints but also sharpen your ability to identify bias, rhetorical strategies, and the strength of different types of arguments. You'll develop a keener sense of how authors convey their stances, which is crucial when analyzing multiple perspectives in reading passages.

Creating a Summary and Predicting Implications

Another valuable drill for enhancing your inference skills is summarizing a passage and predicting its implications. After reading a text, summarize the main idea in just a few sentences. Then, without looking back at the passage, try to predict what logical conclusions or consequences follow from the author's argument. You can ask yourself:

- If the author's argument were true, what else would logically follow?
- What unstated assumptions is the author relying on?
- How might the information in the passage apply in a different context?

This exercise not only solidifies your grasp of the material but also strengthens your ability to think ahead and anticipate potential implications, which is often required in inference questions.

Timed Drills for Improving Speed

Since both inference and analytical questions require deeper thought, time management can be an issue. To improve speed without sacrificing accuracy, you should practice timed drills. Set a timer for short intervals—start with 10 minutes and gradually decrease it to 5 minutes—

and aim to complete a set number of questions within that time frame. This will force you to make quicker inferences and evaluate arguments more efficiently, helping you stay within time limits during the exam.

Improving your performance on inference and analytical questions requires regular and focused practice. By implementing these drills—summarizing texts, comparing perspectives, evaluating arguments, and predicting implications—you will sharpen your ability to draw conclusions, interpret subtle cues, and analyze complex arguments. As you become more comfortable with these practices, you'll develop the skills needed to tackle these questions confidently and accurately within the time constraints.

Reading strategies

Developing effective reading strategies is crucial for tackling different question types, especially under time constraints. Two key strategies, skimming and deep reading, are essential for navigating the reading section. Each serves a distinct purpose: skimming helps you grasp the overall structure and main ideas quickly, while deep reading is reserved for understanding complex details and making inferences. To succeed, you must know when to apply each technique, based on the type of question you're answering.

Skimming: A Strategy for Speed and General Understanding

Skimming is a fast-paced reading technique that allows you to extract the gist of a passage without getting bogged down in every detail. It's especially useful when dealing with main idea or general structure questions, which often ask for an overarching understanding of the text. When skimming, your goal is to capture the main ideas and key points as quickly as possible.

Start by reading the title and any introductory sentences carefully. These elements often contain crucial information about the passage's topic and argument. Then, move on to the first and last sentences of each paragraph. Authors frequently use these sentences to introduce or summarize the main points, which will help you create a mental map of the passage's structure.

For example, if a question asks, "What is the main idea of the passage?" or "Which of the following best summarizes the passage?" skimming can be highly effective. You're not expected to analyze every sentence; rather, focus on the flow of ideas to make an informed guess.

While skimming, it's helpful to keep an eye out for transition words like "however," "therefore," and "in contrast." These signal shifts in the argument, helping you understand how the author develops their points without diving deep into every line.

Deep Reading: A Strategy for Detailed Analysis

On the other hand, deep reading is necessary for questions that require a thorough understanding of specific details, evidence, or complex arguments. In this approach, you engage with the text on a deeper level, analyzing the meaning of individual sentences, paragraphs, and even word choices. This method is slower and more focused, often used for inference or analytical questions, where precision is key.

For example, if a question asks, "What does the author imply about X?" or "According to paragraph three, which of the following statements is true?" deep reading is essential. Here, you're being asked to extract nuanced information that is only available by closely examining the relevant parts of the text.

When practicing deep reading, highlight key sections or underline important phrases that directly relate to the question being asked. It's also important to consider the author's tone and purpose, as these often provide clues for answering inference-based or analytical questions.

Knowing When to Skim and When to Read Deeply

The skill lies in knowing when to apply skimming versus deep reading. Start by reading the questions before you begin the passage. This allows you to know what types of information to look for. If the question is about the passage's main idea or structure, skimming the passage for overall themes will be enough. If the question requires specific details or asks for interpretation, deep reading will be more appropriate.

One common strategy is to skim the entire passage first, just to get an overview, then dive deeper into specific sections that the questions highlight. For example, you might skim to get the passage's main points, then reread particular paragraphs closely if the questions demand further detail.

Balancing Both Approaches for Optimal Performance

Balancing skimming and deep reading ensure that you not only get through the passage quickly but also have the depth of understanding necessary to answer more complex questions. As you practice these techniques, you'll become more adept at determining which strategy to use based on the question type.

For instance, with comparison questions, where you must identify similarities or differences between two ideas presented in the text, skimming is useful for quickly locating relevant sections, but deep reading is required to analyze the subtleties of each argument. Conversely, for factual recall questions, skimming may suffice, as you're simply looking for a specific piece of information.

Both skimming and deep reading are essential reading strategies for different question types. Knowing when to use each method is critical to saving time while ensuring accuracy. Skimming allows you to quickly capture the passage's main ideas and structure, while deep reading gives you the depth needed to tackle detail-oriented or analytical questions. With practice, you'll develop the ability to seamlessly switch between these approaches, improving both speed and comprehension during the reading section.

Chapter 6: Science (Optional): Interpreting Data, Graphs, and Hypotheses

40 minutes for 40 questions: Should you opt-in for the Science section?

The Science section of the exam is now optional, and students face an important choice: whether to opt in for this portion of the test. This decision depends on a variety of factors, including your academic goals, the type of colleges you're applying to, and your comfort with scientific reasoning and data interpretation.

Who Should Consider Taking the Science Section?

First, students aiming for STEM-related fields (Science, Technology, Engineering, Mathematics) or applying to highly competitive programs should seriously consider taking the Science section. Fields like engineering, biology, chemistry, and computer science often require applicants to demonstrate proficiency in scientific reasoning and analysis. Some universities may look for strong performance in this area as part of their admissions decisions, especially for applicants to STEM majors. Although not all schools require this section, submitting strong scores in Science can strengthen your application and showcase your readiness for the rigorous coursework that follows.

Additionally, students who are comfortable analyzing graphs, charts, and data should lean toward opting in for the Science section. This part of the exam is less about content knowledge of scientific facts and more about interpreting data and hypotheses. If you're someone who enjoys solving problems using evidence and data interpretation, then this section might play to your strengths.

Who Might Consider Skipping the Science Section?

If you're applying to programs in fields like humanities, arts, or social sciences, where the emphasis on math and science is lower, you may feel comfortable opting out of the Science section. Admissions for these types of programs often place more importance on your performance in the core sections (English, Reading, and Math) and on non-academic factors like essays and extracurriculars. For these applicants, skipping the Science section allows them to focus their study efforts on areas more relevant to their chosen field.

Additionally, if scientific data interpretation is an area you struggle with or if it causes significant anxiety, opting out of the Science section may relieve unnecessary stress. Since the Science section doesn't require memorizing formulas or complex scientific concepts, many students who are more comfortable with other subjects might prefer to use that energy to maximize their performance in the required sections.

Understanding What the Science Section Tests

The Science section primarily measures scientific reasoning. Students are asked to interpret and analyze data presented in the form of graphs, tables, and charts. There are also questions based on short passages about scientific experiments and hypotheses, which require you to draw conclusions or identify patterns.

For example, you might be asked to interpret the results of an experiment presented in chart form, or to predict the outcome of a hypothesis based on given data. The ability to quickly process visual data and understand the relationship between variables is crucial here.

Time Management in the Science Section

If you decide to opt-in, remember that the section consists of 40 questions in 40 minutes, leaving you with just one minute per question. This tight time frame emphasizes the importance of speed and efficiency when interpreting data. Regular practice with scientific graphs and tables will help you gain familiarity with the types of questions asked and allow you to develop strategies for quickly identifying the key information in each data set.

Weighing the Decision

When deciding whether to take the Science section, consider both your academic goals and personal strengths. If your future ambitions align with science-based fields, taking this section will likely bolster your college applications. However, if you are more focused on the arts or humanities, and feel that your time could be better spent perfecting the other sections, opting out could be the wiser choice.

Ultimately, this decision should be made with a clear understanding of your academic path, the requirements of your target schools, and your own strengths in handling scientific data and reasoning. By weighing these factors carefully, you can make a strategic decision that will help maximize your overall score and increase your chances of college admission success

Understanding scientific reasoning, data interpretation and conflicting viewpoints

Understanding scientific reasoning, data interpretation, and conflicting viewpoints is fundamental to mastering the optional Science section of the test, where you are required to interpret and analyze scientific data. This section tests your ability to think critically, draw conclusions from various data sets, and assess differing hypotheses or scientific opinions.

Scientific Reasoning: The Foundation of Analytical Thinking

Scientific reasoning involves using logic and critical thinking to interpret results, make predictions, and understand relationships between variables. It does not require extensive scientific knowledge but rather the ability to assess the evidence and understand the processes behind experiments. In this context, questions may focus on cause and effect, patterns, and the logical relationships between data sets.

To sharpen your skills in scientific reasoning, it's important to familiarize yourself with experimental design and hypothesis testing. Understanding how an experiment is structured, including the variables (independent and dependent), controls, and methods of data collection, can help you approach questions with greater clarity. For example, a question may ask you to determine how changes in one variable impact another or to predict what might happen if an additional variable is introduced. Learning how to evaluate scientific claims critically, particularly through the lens of data-driven evidence, will strengthen your approach to these questions.

Data Interpretation: Making Sense of Numbers and Visuals

Data interpretation is a critical component of this section, requiring you to read and understand information presented in various forms, such as graphs, charts, and tables. The test may present data that includes numerical figures, trends, and comparisons across different data sets.

When interpreting data, the first step is to identify the key variables and the relationships between them. Are you dealing with a direct correlation between two variables? Is there a pattern in the data over time or across different groups? Often, understanding the trend lines in graphs or the way data points cluster is crucial to answering questions correctly.

Pay attention to labels, scales, and units of measurement on graphs and charts, as these elements can provide important clues. Some questions may ask you to extrapolate beyond the provided data or to identify potential errors in the experimental setup based on the data shown. For example, you might need to predict future outcomes or explain what the data might suggest in an unseen scenario. Developing a quick, systematic way of reviewing and digesting these visual aids will enhance your ability to answer such questions swiftly and accurately.

Conflicting Viewpoints: Comparing Hypotheses

One unique aspect of the Science section involves conflicting viewpoints, where multiple scientists or researchers present differing hypotheses or interpretations of the same data. These questions test your ability to compare, contrast, and assess the validity of each viewpoint. You'll often be required to identify points of agreement, disagreement, and ambiguity between the different perspectives.

Conflicting viewpoint passages typically present two or more theories or explanations, often without a clear right or wrong answer. The challenge here lies in understanding how each scientist interprets the available data and what assumptions or evidence they are using to support their hypothesis. You might be asked to explain why one scientist supports a particular conclusion based on the same data that another scientist interprets differently.

To tackle these questions, focus on identifying the core arguments of each viewpoint and how they rely on the evidence presented. Pay close attention to the language used—scientists might use qualifiers like "likely" or "possibly" to hedge their conclusions, indicating that their argument isn't fully conclusive. Recognizing these subtle differences helps you evaluate the strength of each argument.

Integrating These Skills

Ultimately, mastering scientific reasoning, data interpretation and the analysis of conflicting viewpoints requires consistent practice with a variety of scientific scenarios. You'll need to balance speed with accuracy, as the section is tightly timed. Working through practice questions that mimic these challenges will help you recognize patterns and improve your critical thinking skills.

Understanding how to think like a scientist - analyzing evidence, drawing reasoned conclusions, and critically evaluating differing viewpoints - is the key to performing well in this section. Whether or not you opt for the Science section, these analytical skills are invaluable for academic success and real-world problem-solving.

Charts, graphs and tables

Analyzing charts, graphs and tables is a fundamental skill for interpreting data efficiently, especially in sections where scientific reasoning is tested. These visual representations of data provide a concise way to present complex information, allowing you to draw conclusions, identify trends, and make comparisons quickly. Developing a strategy to analyze these visuals efficiently is essential for success.

Understanding the Basics

Before diving into the analysis, it's crucial to have a solid grasp of the basic elements that make up charts, graphs, and tables. Whether it's a bar chart, line graph, scatter plot, or table, certain components are consistent across all types of data displays:

- Axes (for graphs): These typically represent variables. The x-axis might show time or a category, while the y-axis usually represents a measurement or result.
- Labels and Titles: These provide context about the data, including what is being measured and how.

- Scales and Units: Pay attention to the units of measurement (e.g., seconds, millimeters, kilograms) and the scale used. Scales can be linear or logarithmic, and understanding this is essential for interpreting the data accurately.
- Data Points and Patterns: Look for the specific values plotted, whether as bars, points, or other markers, and note any apparent patterns or trends.
- Legends (for multi-variable graphs): In charts that involve multiple variables, a legend is crucial for identifying the different data sets.

Analyzing Graphs

When analyzing line graphs or scatter plots, your main focus should be on the relationship between variables. For instance, does one variable increase as the other decreases (negative correlation), or do they both increase (positive correlation)? Spotting these trends is the first step in interpreting the graph's message.

For example, in a line graph, look at how the line progresses over time or across categories. Is there a steady increase, a decrease, or fluctuations? In scientific contexts, these changes might represent the results of an experiment or a pattern that needs to be explained.

For scatter plots, you should look for the distribution of points. Do they form a cluster? Do they seem to follow a certain trajectory? These visual cues will help you understand if there's a relationship between the variables plotted and how strong or weak that relationship might be.

Analyzing Bar and Pie Charts

Bar charts are ideal for comparing discrete data points across categories. When analyzing a bar chart, your goal is to quickly assess the differences in height between bars. The taller the bar, the greater the value it represents. Pay close attention to both the x-axis (categories) and y-axis (values) to understand what's being compared.

Pie charts, on the other hand, show proportions. Your focus here should be on which segments are the largest and how the data is divided overall. This type of chart is less common in rigorous scientific settings but might appear in cases involving proportionate data, such as population studies or percentages.

Analyzing Tables

Tables provide numerical data in a structured format. While they may seem less visual than charts or graphs, they still contain a wealth of information if you approach them correctly. Start by reading the table's title and labels carefully to understand the variables involved. Next, scan through the columns and rows to identify trends or outliers.

One effective way to approach tables is to look for maxima and minima—the highest and lowest values in each column or row. This allows you to quickly pinpoint key data points without getting lost in the numbers. You might also want to compare averages or totals across different categories, depending on what the question asks.

Common Pitfalls and How to Avoid Them

One common mistake when analyzing charts, graphs, or tables is misreading the axes or labels. Always check the scales carefully—sometimes graphs use non-standard intervals or logarithmic scales that can throw off your interpretation if you're not paying attention. Similarly, ensure you understand what the different symbols or colors represent, especially if there is more than one variable in play.

Another pitfall is focusing too much on specific data points without considering the overall trend. While details are important, the bigger picture often reveals the most useful information, especially when answering questions that ask about general patterns or hypotheses.

Time Management Tips

Given the tight time constraints, it's important to approach each chart, graph, or table with a clear plan. First, glance over the entire visual to get a sense of what's being presented. Then, quickly locate the key data points that relate to the question at hand. Don't spend too much time trying to understand every detail unless the question specifically asks for it. Instead, focus on the aspects that directly affect your answer.

Efficiently analyzing charts, graphs, and tables requires a balance of understanding the basic components, spotting trends and patterns, and managing your time effectively. With regular practice, you'll develop the ability to interpret these visual data formats quickly and accurately, allowing you to answer questions confidently while staying within the time limit. This skill is not only essential for the exam but also applicable in many real-world situations where interpreting data is crucial.

The importance of the Science section for STEM applicants

For students aiming to pursue a degree in STEM (Science, Technology, Engineering, and Mathematics), the Science section plays a crucial role in demonstrating their readiness for rigorous college-level coursework. Although this section has been made optional in the updated version of the test, opting to include it can offer significant advantages for those interested in STEM fields. It allows students to showcase their skills in scientific reasoning, data analysis, and the ability to interpret complex experiments and hypotheses — all of which are essential in STEM programs.

STEM disciplines are rooted in data analysis, scientific inquiry, and critical thinking. The Science section provides an opportunity for students to exhibit these skills. Unlike traditional science tests that focus on recalling facts, this section emphasizes scientific reasoning and problem-solving. Students are expected to interpret data from graphs, tables, and charts, analyze scientific experiments, and evaluate hypotheses and conflicting viewpoints. This process mirrors the kind of analytical thinking required in STEM courses, from physics and chemistry to engineering and data science.

For universities that place a strong emphasis on STEM education, strong performance in the Science section signals that an applicant has both the intellectual ability and mindset required to succeed in these demanding programs. Admissions officers can see that the student is well-prepared to handle scientific content, not just through coursework, but through the ability to think critically and draw accurate conclusions based on experimental data.

In competitive college admissions, particularly for STEM programs, students are often evaluated based on their demonstrated ability in science and math. Opting for the Science section adds another data point for colleges to assess, providing a fuller picture of the applicant's capabilities. Even if a school does not explicitly require this section, a strong score can bolster an application, especially if the student is aiming for a program that values quantitative and analytical skills.

Additionally, many STEM fields are highly competitive. Whether it's applying for an engineering program at a top university or pursuing a degree in environmental science, students often find themselves competing with peers who have similar academic records and extracurricular achievements. Performing well in the Science section can help distinguish an applicant from others with comparable qualifications, offering a competitive edge that could be crucial during the admissions process.

STEM programs are known for their challenging curriculum, where students are expected to interpret complex scientific information, solve multi-step problems, and critically evaluate research findings. The Science section mimics this kind of thinking. It focuses on understanding experimental setups, analyzing data, and drawing conclusions, all of which reflect the demands of higher education in STEM.

By choosing to include the Science section in their testing, students essentially give themselves a practice run for the type of work they will encounter in college. It serves as a preview of what will be expected in university laboratories, research projects, and lectures. In fact, developing proficiency in interpreting scientific data and reasoning will make the transition to college-level STEM courses smoother, offering a head start in academic preparedness.

For many students, STEM careers are the ultimate goal. Fields like engineering, biotechnology, and data science rely heavily on the ability to interpret data and evaluate scientific problems. The skills tested in the Science section, such as analyzing complex data sets and making evidence-based decisions, align with what is required in these professions.

Taking the Science section not only strengthens a student's college application but also helps to foster the kinds of thinking required in STEM careers. Whether analyzing medical data, creating engineering models, or interpreting ecological research, the skills gained from mastering scientific reasoning and data analysis will be directly applicable in the professional world.

While the Science section is now optional, it remains an important part of the test for students aiming for STEM programs. By demonstrating strong scientific reasoning and data interpretation skills, students can gain a competitive edge in college admissions and prepare for the academic challenges they will face in STEM disciplines. For those serious about pursuing careers in fields such as engineering, medicine, or environmental science, the Science section offers a valuable opportunity to showcase their strengths and align their test performance with their long-term goals.

Chapter 7: Preparing for ACT Success – Practice and Review

Practice Test 1: English section

1. In the sentence below, which of the following subordinating conjunctions will MOST change the meaning of the sentence when substituted for the underlined "if"?

That bear won't attack us _if_ we lay down and play dead.

- o   after
- o   unless
- o   once
- o   if only

2. Choose the answer that best corrects the underlined portion of the sentence. If the underlined portion is correct as written, choose "NO CHANGE."

Neither Danny _or_ Rebecca was adequately prepared for the tennis match that afternoon.

- o   either
- o   nor
- o   also
- o   NO CHANGE
- o   and

3. Choose the answer that best corrects the underlined portion of the sentence. If the underlined portion is correct as written, choose "NO CHANGE."

We enjoyed going to Alice's art class, _and_ the long drive over was starting to become a deterrent.

- o   but
- o   NO CHANGE
- o   therefore
- o   and then
- o   also

4. Choose the answer that best corrects the underlined portion of the sentence. If the underlined portion is correct as written, choose "NO CHANGE."

My first task of the day was <u>watch</u> that black-and-white Italian film once again.

- ○ watched
- ○ to watch
- ○ will watch
- ○ NO CHANGE
- ○ having watched

5. Choose the answer that best corrects the underlined portion of the sentence. If the underlined portion is correct as written, choose "NO CHANGE."

As Amad and Sarah walked down the street, <u>they had found a penny</u> lying on the concrete.

- ○ they found a penny
- ○ they were finding a penny
- ○ they had finding a penny
- ○ NO CHANGE
- ○ they find a penny

6. Choose the answer that best corrects the underlined portion of the sentence. If the underlined portion is correct as written, choose "NO CHANGE."

Susan <u>has went</u> to the book store to buy the texts she needed for the semester.

- ○ gone
- ○ had went
- ○ goes
- ○ NO CHANGE
- ○ went

7. Choose the answer that best corrects the underlined portion of the sentence. If the underlined portion is correct as written, choose "NO CHANGE."

If I <u>were</u> a teacher, I would grade fairly.

- ○ can be
- ○ NO CHANGE
- ○ am ever
- ○ have been
- ○ was

8. Choose the answer that best corrects the underlined portion of the sentence. If the underlined portion is correct as written, choose "NO CHANGE."

Hans had fallen <u>quick</u> when the wind caught his ladder.

- ○ quicker
- ○ pretty quick
- ○ NO CHANGE
- ○ quickest
- ○ quickly

9. Choose the answer that best corrects the underlined portion of the sentence. If the underlined portion is correct as written, choose "NO CHANGE."

She was <u>surprisingly quick</u> on the uptake.

- ○ NO CHANGE
- ○ surprised quick
- ○ quick
- ○ surprised quickly
- ○ surprisingly quickly

10. Choose the answer that best corrects the underlined portion of the sentence. If the underlined portion is correct as written, choose "NO CHANGE."

Aerin's <u>beautiful written</u> speech brought tears to the eyes of his fellow classmates at graduation.

- ○ beautiful wrote
- ○ beautifully
- ○ beautifully written
- ○ beautifully wrote
- ○ NO CHANGE

11. Choose the answer that best corrects the underlined portion of the sentence. If the underlined portion is correct as written, choose "NO CHANGE."

It's a general rule that the temperatures in spring differ <u>with</u> the temperatures in winter, though there are some exceptions.

- ○ by
- ○ NO CHANGE
- ○ as
- ○ without
- ○ from

12. Choose the answer that best corrects the underlined portion of the sentence. If the underlined portion is correct as written, choose "NO CHANGE."

<u>"That's not the way you would write that!," she exclaimed.</u>

- ○ "That's not the way you would write that!" she exclaimed!
- ○ NO CHANGE

- o "That's not the way you would write that," she exclaimed!
- o "That's not the way you would write that," she exclaimed.
- o "That's not the way you would write that!" she exclaimed.

13. Choose the answer that best corrects the underlined portion of the sentence. If the underlined portion is correct as written, choose "NO CHANGE."

Sawyer attended <u>that high school his first</u> solo violin performance took place in the auditorium during his sophomore year.

- o NO CHANGE
- o that high school, but his first
- o that high school, his first
- o that high school; his first
- o that high school? His first

14. Choose the answer that best corrects the underlined portion of the sentence. If the underlined portion is correct as written, choose "NO CHANGE."

<u>James chose a large, rusty car, Philip chose a brand-new car, and I chose the cheapest, ugliest car on the lot.</u>

- o James chose a large, rusty car; Philip chose a brand-new car; and I chose the cheapest, ugliest car on the lot.
- o James chose a large, rusty car, Philip chose a brand-new car; and I chose the cheapest, ugliest car on the lot.
- o NO CHANGE
- o James chose a large rusty car, Philip chose a brand-new car, and I chose the cheapest ugliest car on the lot.
- o James chose a large rusty car Philip chose a brand-new car and I chose the cheapest ugliest car on the lot.

15. Choose the answer that best corrects the underlined portion of the sentence. If the underlined portion is correct as written, choose "NO CHANGE."

The sun was blotted out as thousands of <u>birds silhouettes</u> appeared overhead.

- o birds' silhouettes
- o NO CHANGE
- o bird's silhouettes'
- o birds silhouette's
- o bird's silhouettes

16. Choose the answer that best corrects the underlined portion of the sentence. If the underlined portion is correct as written, choose "NO CHANGE."

<u>The Emperor Augustus dog has the sniffles.</u>

- ○ The Emperor Augustuses dog has the sniffles.
- ○ NO CHANGE
- ○ The Emperor Augustu's dog has the sniffles.
- ○ The Emperor Augustus' dog has the sniffles.
- ○ The Emperor Augustus' dog's have the sniffles.

17. Choose the answer that best corrects the underlined portion of the sentence. If the underlined portion is correct as written, choose "NO CHANGE."

A few guests' bags had been stolen that night.

- ○ of the guest's
- ○ NO CHANGE
- ○ guests
- ○ guest
- ○ guest's

18. Choose the answer that best corrects the underlined portion of the sentence. If the underlined portion is correct as written, choose "NO CHANGE."

The best ingredients for a BLT are: bacon, lettuce, tomato, toasted bread, and mayo.

- ○ The best ingredients for a BLT: bacon, lettuce, tomato, toasted bread, and mayo.
- ○ The best ingredient for a BLT is: bacon, lettuce, tomato, toasted bread, and mayo.
- ○ The best ingredients for a BLT are bacon, lettuce, tomato, toasted bread, and mayo.
- ○ NO CHANGE
- ○ The best ingredients for a BLT are, bacon, lettuce, tomato, toasted bread, and mayo.

19. Choose the answer that best corrects the underlined portion of the sentence. If the underlined portion is correct as written, choose "NO CHANGE."

While they are both great pastry chefs, Eric's chocolate chip cookies are definitely better than Henry.

- ○ NO CHANGE
- ○ Henry's
- ○ Henrys'
- ○ Henrys
- ○ that by Henry

20. Choose the answer that best corrects the underlined portion of the passage. If the underlined portion is correct as written, choose "NO CHANGE."

The Chunnel actually consists of three tunnels: a southern tunnel, a northern tunnel, and a service tunnel in the middle. The southern tunnel carries passengers from France to England, while the northern tunnel carries people from England to France. The service tunnel serves as an escape route in case of emergency and also allows workers to enter the tunnel to perform routine maintenance.

- including a south tunnel, north tunnel, and a tunnel for service
- two tunnels, which are southern and northern, and another tunnel
- one southern tunnel, a northern tunnel, and a service tunnel
- NO CHANGE
- a southern tunnel, a north tunnel, and another tunnel, a service tunnel

21. Choose the answer that best corrects the underlined portion of the sentence. If the underlined portion is correct as written, choose "NO CHANGE."

My three favorite activities are <u>skateboarding, to swim, and playing golf.</u>

- skateboarding, swimming, and playing golf
- skateboarding to swim and playing golf
- skateboard, swimming, and playing golf
- NO CHANGE
- skateboard, swim, and play golf

22. Choose the answer that best corrects the underlined portion of the sentence. If the underlined portion is correct as written, choose "NO CHANGE."

A group of travelers in the hotel lobby <u>seem</u> to be ready for breakfast.

- seems
- have seemed
- NO CHANGE
- are seeming
- to seem

23. Choose the answer that best corrects the underlined portion of the sentence. If the underlined portion is correct as written, choose "NO CHANGE."

There <u>was</u> a team of ice skaters gathered in the hotel lobby earlier today.

- are
- is
- were
- NO CHANGE
- has been

24. Choose the answer that best corrects the underlined portion of the sentence. If the underlined portion is correct as written, choose "NO CHANGE."

Bob and Joe were so hungry that a whole pizza might not have satisfied <u>his</u> hunger.

- he's
- its
- their

- ○ there
- ○ NO CHANGE

25. Which of the following, if any, would NOT be an acceptable substitution for the underlined word?

As the two cars <u>collided</u> into each other, the drivers' airbags deployed with a loud bang.

- ○ crashed
- ○ slammed
- ○ intersected
- ○ smashed
- ○ plowed

26. In order to make this paragraph as logical as possible, where should Sentence 2 be placed?

[1] Today, passengers can travel through the 31-mile tunnel in just 20 minutes. [2] However, cars cannot drive through the tunnel. [3] While some people choose to ride on passenger trains, it is also possible to travel via car. [4] Instead, cars must be driven onto special trains. [5] Passengers then remain in their cars during the journey, and upon reaching the station, they simply drive their cars off the train.

- ○ Before Sentence 1
- ○ After Sentence 5
- ○ Where it is now
- ○ After Sentence 4
- ○ After Sentence 3

27. Choose the answer that best corrects the underlined portion of the sentence. If the underlined portion is correct as written, choose "NO CHANGE."

At that school on Fridays, the <u>childrens' lunches</u> are made by a local seafood chef who makes crowd favorites like California roll sushi and fried popcorn shrimp.

- ○ NO CHANGE
- ○ childs' lunches
- ○ childrens lunch's
- ○ childrens lunches
- ○ children's lunches

28. Choose the answer that best corrects the bolded portion of the passage. If the bolded portion is correct as written, choose "NO CHANGE."

Communist rule in Poland ended <u>in 1989 and</u> the following year proved disastrous for the Polish economy. Prices rapidly ballooned while incomes dropped. Attempting to find a solution, <u>the Balcerowicz Plan was implemented by Polish officials</u>. The plan

liberalized the economy by abolishing price controls, exposing markets to international competition, and it discontinued most industrial subsidies. **In the time of the years following these efforts**, economic growth has **increased steady**.

After years of negotiations and economic and political reforms, Poland became a member of The European Union on May 1, 2004. Soon after, Polish officials voted in favor for laws that would eventually mend the unemployment problem in Poland significantly. In fact, the unemployment rate improved for the first time in five years immediately following Poland's membership. The involvement of Poland in the Eastern Bloc is currently greater than the Czech Republic. The passage of two policies regarding energy credits from foreign countries provide evidence of the emergence of Poland in the global economy.

- o   The years since the time of these efforts
- o   In the years following these efforts
- o   NO CHANGE
- o   In the time since the years following these efforts
- o   During the years that spanned the time immediately following these efforts

29. Which of the following would NOT be an acceptable alternative to the underlined portion of the passage?

Although the tunnel would make it significantly easier to travel between the two countries, people in England were hesitant. Prior to the construction of the Chunnel, England could not be reached via land, and the British were worried that the construction of the tunnel would allow illegal immigrants to enter the country. They also feared that the tunnel would make it easier for invading countries to attack. **Nonetheless**, a plan for the tunnel was created in 1856, and drilling began in 1880.

- o   Additionally
- o   Regardless
- o   Nevertheless
- o   Despite this
- o   Still

30. Choose the answer that best corrects the underlined portion of the sentence. If the underlined portion is correct as written, choose "NO CHANGE."

Allison packed twelve cans of soda for the trip, but her father told her she'd selected **two many cans** to fit in the cooler.

- o   two much cans
- o   too many cans
- o   NO CHANGE
- o   too much cans
- o   too many can's

31. Choose the answer that best corrects the underlined portion of the sentence. If the underlined portion is correct as written, choose "NO CHANGE."

When she was asked what her favorite activity was, Micaela <u>said sleep</u>.

- ○ said "sleeping."
- ○ says "sleep."
- ○ says "sleeping."
- ○ "slept."
- ○ NO CHANGE

32. Choose the answer that best corrects the underlined portion of the sentence. If the underlined portion is correct as written, choose "NO CHANGE."

The witness turned and pointed a shaky finger at the <u>person that had fired</u> the gun into the air.

- ○ person who had fired
- ○ person that fired
- ○ NO CHANGE
- ○ person whom had fired
- ○ person which had fired

33. Choose the answer that best corrects the underlined portion of the sentence. If the underlined portion is correct as written, choose "NO CHANGE."

After the party, Maria, <u>who the party was thrown for</u>, walked home alone, savoring the memories of the friends she would be leaving when she moved for her new job next week.

- ○ for whose the party was thrown
- ○ for who the party was thrown
- ○ for whom the party was thrown
- ○ for whom the party was thrown for
- ○ NO CHANGE

34. Choose the answer that best corrects the underlined portion of the passage. If the underlined portion is correct as written, choose "NO CHANGE."

The Channel Tunnel is a feat of engineering. After <u>decades</u> of discussion, planning, and construction, a project that was first conceived in 1802 has finally become a reality. Today, the Chunnel allows millions of people to travel easily between England and France.

- ○ NO CHANGE
- ○ a ton
- ○ decades and many years

- o tens of years
- o a number of decades

35. Choose the answer that best corrects the underlined portion of the passage. If the underlined portion is correct as written, choose "NO CHANGE."

Unfortunately, two years later, the public fear of invasion won out, and the digging stopped. Almost 100 years later, in 1973, investigations into building a tunnel began again, but once more, digging stopped after two years. This time, <u>construction on the tunnel was prevented in England by economic continued recession</u>. Finally, in 1984, construction began on what eventually became the Chunnel. In 1987, workers began digging on the British side; the following year, digging on the French side began.

- o continued construction on the tunnel was prevented, by an economic recession, in England
- o NO CHANGE
- o an economic recession in England prevented continued construction on the tunnel
- o an economic recession—in England—prevented continued construction on the tunnel
- o continued construction in England on the tunnel prevented by an economic recession

36. Choose the answer that best corrects the underlined portion of the passage. If the underlined portion is correct as written, choose "NO CHANGE."

<u>I love to cleaning</u>. It's a good way to unwind at the end of the day, and, I always function better in a clean environment. I once heard someone say, "You're home is your temple." I attempt to lived my life by that. My priorities are getting rid of clutter, sweeping the floor, washing the dishes, and cleaning the counter top in our kitchen. I mop the floor extremely, quickly. I don't mop all that often, but my roommates appreciate it whenever I do!.

- o I loved cleaning.
- o NO CHANGE
- o I love when to cleaning.
- o I love cleaning.
- o I love when cleaning.

37. Choose the answer that best corrects the underlined portion of the sentence. If the underlined portion is correct as written, choose "NO CHANGE".

Because it's a federal holiday, neither the post office <u>or</u> the bank will be open on Monday.

- o and
- o NO CHANGE
- o nor even
- o nor
- o and not even

38. Choose the answer that best corrects the underlined portion of the sentence. If the underlined portion is correct as written, choose "NO CHANGE."

Every Thursday night, Eric, Alex, <u>and me</u> get together to see a movie.

- o   and me;
- o   and I;
- o   NO CHANGE
- o   and me,
- o   and I

39. Choose the answer that best corrects the underlined portion of the sentence. If the underlined portion is correct as written, choose "NO CHANGE."

Two things I knew for <u>certain</u>; she was not who she said she was, and I was in danger.

- o   certain: and
- o   certainly:
- o   certain,
- o   certain:
- o   NO CHANGE

40. Choose the answer that best corrects the underlined portion of the sentence. If the underlined portion is correct as written, choose "NO CHANGE."

The <u>sky which was black and stormy</u> virtually guaranteed a snow day from school.

- o   sky, which was black and stormy,
- o   sky, which was black, and stormy,
- o   NO CHANGE
- o   sky which was black and stormy,
- o   sky, which was black and stormy

41. Choose the answer that best corrects the underlined portion of the sentence. If the underlined portion is correct as written, choose "NO CHANGE."

Sometimes it is better to forgive and <u>forget, then</u> to hold grudges.

- o   forget then
- o   NO CHANGES
- o   forget
- o   forget, but
- o   forget than

42. Choose the answer that best corrects the underlined portion of the sentence. If the underlined portion is correct as written, choose "NO CHANGE."

<u>One of his classes meets at 8 a.m., but he has another at 8 p.m.</u>

- ○ NO CHANGE
- ○ One of his classes meets at 8 a.m, but he has another at 8 p.m.
- ○ One of his classes meets at 8 a.m., but he has another at 8 p.m..
- ○ One of his classes meets at 8 a.m. but he has another at 8 p.m.
- ○ One of his classes meets at 8 a,m, but he has another at 8 p,m.

43. Identify the prepositional phrase(s) in the sentence below.

A cold wind from the north cut through the woods, making the air outside the tent unbearably cold.

- ○ through the woods
- ○ None of these answers
- ○ from the north
- ○ outside the tent
- ○ All of these answers

44. Choose the answer that best corrects the underlined portion of the sentence. If the underlined portion is correct as written, choose "NO CHANGE."

The failing grade I received on my last test was the <u>result of</u> not studying enough.

- ○ result by
- ○ result which
- ○ NO CHANGE
- ○ result to
- ○ result for

45. Choose the answer that best corrects the underlined portion of the sentence. If the underlined portion is correct as written, choose "NO CHANGE."

<u>The dog went to it's doghouse and proceeded to bury all of it's belongings.</u>

- ○ NO CHANGE
- ○ The dog gone to its doghouse and proceded to bury all of its belongings.
- ○ The dog went to doghouse and proceeded to bury all of belongings.
- ○ The dog went to its doghouse and proceeded to bury all of its belongings.
- ○ The dog went to its' doghouse and proceeded to bury all of its' belongings.

46. Choose the answer that best corrects the underlined portion of the sentence. If the underlined portion is correct as written, choose "NO CHANGE."

Seeing the stable had always been Madeleine's favorite part of visiting her grandparents; it had been her <u>family's</u> for nearly a century and the architecture reflected a time long past.

- ○ NO CHANGE

- o familie's
- o families'
- o familys'
- o families

47. Choose the answer that best corrects the underlined portion of the sentence. If the underlined portion is correct as written, choose "NO CHANGE."

Did someone in here shout "Fire"?

- o Did someone in here shout "Fire"!
- o NO CHANGE
- o Did someone in here shout "Fire!"?
- o Did someone in here shout fire?
- o Did someone in here shout "Fire"?!

48. Choose the answer that best corrects the underlined portion of the passage. If the underlined portion is correct as written, choose "NO CHANGE."

Weighing more than 15,000 tons each, workers used massive tunnel boring machines to dig the tunnel. Each one could cut through the earth at a rate of approximately 15 feet per hour. These machines also collected the spoil, or earth removed by the machines, and sent it out of the tunnel via a long conveyer belt. A concrete lining was also added to the tunnel to prevent it from collapsing. To ensure that the French and British teams would eventually meet in the middle, the tunnel boring machines were steered using lasers.

- o Which weighed more than 15,000 tons each, workers dug the tunnel using massive tunnel boring machines.
- o Weighing more than 15,000 tons each, workers dug the tunnel using massive tunnel boring machines.
- o Weighing more than 15,000 tons each, massive tunnel boring machines were used to dig the tunnel.
- o NO CHANGE
- o More than 15,000 tons each, workers used massive tunnel boring machines to dig the tunnel.

49. Choose the answer that best corrects the underlined portion of the sentence. If the underlined portion is correct as written, choose "NO CHANGE."

Unlike most high school students, Alex prefers to knit, sew, and creating costumes for his pets on the weekends.

- o to knit, sew, and create costumes
- o to knit, to sew, and creating
- o to knit, sew and creating costumes
- o knitting, sewing, and to create costumes
- o NO CHANGE

50. Choose the answer that best corrects the underlined portion of the sentence. If the underlined portion is correct as written, choose "NO CHANGE."

The new law was passed by a two-thirds majority.

- o NO CHANGE
- o A two-thirds majority passes the new law.
- o A two-thirds majority passed the new law.
- o The new law is passed by a two-thirds majority.
- o The new law was passing by a two-thirds majority.

Answer sheet with explanation

1. **Correct Answer**: unless

Explanation: Of all of the possible subordinating conjunctions provided as answer choices, only "unless" makes it sound as though lying down and playing dead will result in the bear attacking. The other answers all make the opposite recommendation. So, "unless" most changes the meaning of the sentence and is thus the correct answer.

2. **Correct Answer**: nor

Explanation: "Neither" is paired with "nor," "either" is paired with "or." "Neither Danny nor Rebecca" is the correct grammatical pairing in this situation.

3. **Correct Answer**: but

Explanation: The first and second parts of the sentence are both independent clauses. Since they demonstrate a contrast (We like going to the class BUT the drive is too long), "but" is the correct conjunction in this sentence.

4. **Correct Answer**: to watch

Explanation: The "task" requires the infinitive of the verb in order to be grammatically correct. It helps to break down the sentence to its basics: "My first task was to watch."

5. **Correct Answer**: they found a penny

Explanation: The correct answer is the only one which matches the tense of the rest of the sentence. NO CHANGE would be correct if the tense were past progressive ("were walking"), but this is not the case.

6. **Correct Answer**: went

Explanation: The correct past tense of "go" is "went."

7. **Correct Answer**: NO CHANGE

Explanation: This is the proper usage of the subjunctive mood. In this instance, the speaker is not (and has presumably never been) a teacher, but is instead thinking about the potential scenario. When working with hypotheticals, the subjunctive is the correct case.

8. **Correct Answer**: quickly

Explanation: The word "quickly" is an adverb that is used to modify the verb "fallen" (by explaining HOW the falling had taken place).

9. **Correct Answer**: NO CHANGE

Explanation: The sentence is correct as is. "Surprisingly" is an adverb modifying the verb, "quick," so it correctly ends in "-ly." The other options change the meaning of the sentence.

10. **Correct Answer**: beautifully written

Explanation: The adverb necessary here is "beautifully," which modifies the past participle, "written." Participles are verbs acting as adjectives.
Adverbs can modify verbs or adjectives.

11. **Correct Answer**: from

Explanation: This is an idiomatic usage of a preposition. There is not necessarily a rule for the correct usage here, other than what is commonly accepted in the English language. It helps to read the sentence aloud in order to identify which options sound incorrect.

12. **Correct Answer**: "That's not the way you would write that!" she exclaimed.

Explanation: The phrase "she exclaimed" necessitates the use of the exclamation mark, which takes the place of the comma that normally goes inside quotation marks at the end of a quoted sentence. The sentence itself is not an exclamation, though. It is the person being quoted who is over-excited, not the person reporting what she has said.

13. **Correct Answer**: that high school; his first

Explanation: Unchanged, the presented sentence is a run-on. The option "that high school, his first" does not fix it completely as it is a comma splice. The option "that high school, but his first" does join the two independent clauses, but it is incorrect as it indicates the two clauses contradict each other. The correct answer, "that high school; his first" correctly joins the two related independent clauses with a semicolon.

14. **Correct Answer**: James chose a large, rusty car; Philip chose a brand new car; and I chose the cheapest, ugliest car on the lot.

Explanation: Because the first and third clauses in this sentence contain commas themselves, semicolons are needed to separate the clauses in order to avoid confusion. Also, because the phrases
"large, rusty car" and "cheapest, ugliest car" can also be rendered as "large and rusty car" and "cheapest and ugliest car", the commas separating the adjectives are necessary.

15. **Correct Answer**: birds' silhouettes

Explanation: Only the correct answer shows proper possession of the noun "silhouettes" by the plural noun "birds." Remember, the singular or plural nature of a noun is often revealed through context clues (in this case, the word "thousands").

16. **Correct Answer**: The Emperor Augustus' dog has the sniffles.

Explanation: "The Emperor Augustus' dog has the sniffles" is the correct answer. When forming a possessive with a proper noun that ends in -s, such as "Augustus," the apostrophe follows the -s. (You may see some style guides give "Augustus's dog" as the correct answer for a problem like this, but this way of forming the possessive is falling out of favor.) American readers will read the phrase aloud as "Augustuses dog", whereas British readers will read it aloud as "Augustus dog", but both will use the apostrophe after the -s.

17. **Correct Answer**: NO CHANGE

Explanation: An apostrophe denotes possession. In this case, the bags belong to a few guests. Because the noun "guests" is plural, the apostrophe is placed after the "s." If it were only one guest (if the noun were singular), then the apostrophe would be placed before the "s."

18. **Correct Answer**: The best ingredients for a BLT are bacon, lettuce, tomato, toasted bread, and mayo.

Explanation: No colon is needed for a list that is grammatically part of the sentence, so the correct answer is "The best ingredients for a BLT are bacon, lettuce, tomato, toasted bread, and mayo." Colons are only used in lists when the list is attached to a complete sentence, as in "The best ingredients for a BLT are as follows: bacon, lettuce, tomato, toasted bread, and mayo," but they would not be used in sentence fragments such as "The best ingredients for a BLT: bacon, lettuce, tomato, toasted bread, and mayo."

19. **Correct Answer**: Henry's

Explanation: It is incorrect to compare Eric's cookies to Henry; they are two different things. You can only compare Eric's cookies and Henry's cookies, and the most efficient way to do so is by saying "Henry's."

20. **Correct Answer**: NO CHANGE

Explanation: The correct choice incorporates parallel structure effectively. In this case, each tunnel is preceded by "a," and the first two both have an "-ern" ending ("southern" and "northern").

21. **Correct Answer**: skateboarding, swimming, and playing golf

Explanation: The three activities are in a list, so commas must separate them. Thus, "skateboarding, to swim, and playing golf" is incorrect. Also, to achieve parallel structure, each item on the list must be written in the same form. In this case, because "skateboarding" and "playing golf" are gerunds, or verbs that end in "-ing" acting as nouns. "To swim" is written in the infinite form, though, so "to swim" should be changed to its gerund form, "swimming."

22. **Correct Answer**: seems

Explanation: "Seems" matches both the tense of the sentence (present) and case of the subject, "a group," which is singular. "Seem" may seem correct, but the verb here describes the "group" as one whole, rather than describing a plural group of travelers. "Travelers" cannot be the subject of the sentence because it is contained in a prepositional phrase and unnecessary to the sentence's structure.
If you find this confusing, try omitting the prepositional phrase from the sentence: "A group in the hotel lobby seem to be ready for breakfast" makes the error more apparent.

23. **Correct Answer**: NO CHANGE

Explanation: "A team" is singular, so we need to pick out a singular verb. We also need that verb to be in the past tense so that it matches the past tense verb "gathered" that appears later in the sentence and makes sense given the phrase "earlier today." The verb that is written in the sentence as-is, "was," is the only answer choice that fulfills both of these criteria, so "NO CHANGE" is the correct answer.

24 **Correct Answer**: their

Explanation: The pronoun has to match the subject. Since the subject is compound ("Bob and Joe"), the pronoun must be plural.

25. **Correct Answer**: intersected

Explanation: Only the word "intersected" does not need to be followed by "into".
In addition, the word "intersected" sounds overly formal when compared to the tone of the other three choices and the original verb.

26. **Correct Answer**: After Sentence

Explanation: "However" suggests a contrast. The logical contrast in this paragraph is the contrast between the statement that it is possible to take a car through the tunnel and the statement that the car cannot simply be driven through the tunnel.

27. **Correct Answer**: children's lunches

Explanation: " The lunches belong to the children, so the correct possessive is "children's"; the "lunches" are simply plural.

28. **Correct Answer**: In the years following these efforts

Explanation: The phrase "In the time of the years following these efforts" is redundant because years are always a unit of time, so having both 'years" and "time" is unnecessary. The more concise way to express the idea is "In the years following these efforts."
None of the other answer choices express the idea of the sentence —that economic growth showed signs of improvement following the implementation of the plan-without introducing redundancy.

29. **Correct Answer**: Additionally

Explanation: The word "Although" at the beginning of the paragraph sets up two contrasting ideas. In this case, the tunnel was built despite many fears.

30. **Correct Answer**: too many cans

Explanation: "Drinks" can be counted, making them a countable noun, unlike a noun like "water," which isn't countable. (You wouldn't say "two water" but you might say "two drinks.") "Too many" is used to refer to countable nouns. "Drinks" is a plural noun and the drinks are not possessing anything, so "too many drinks" is the correct answer.

31. **Correct Answer**: said "sleeping."

Explanation: Instead of the noun "sleep," a better choice is the gerund "sleeping". A gerund is a verb that ends in "-ing," like a participle, but acts like a noun (instead of an adjective). In this situation where Micaela is asked about an activity, it's better to use the gerund form because it is more "active" than just the normal noun.

32. **Correct Answer**: person who had fired

Explanation: "Who" is used for people. "That" and "which" are used for things. In addition, "person that fired" changes the tense of the verb "fired," and introduces confusion into the sentence.

33. **Correct Answer**: for whom the party was thrown

Explanation: In this clause, the party is thrown for Maria, so she is an object and not the subject of the clause. "Who" is used to refer to the subject and is therefore incorrect. "Who ... for" is also incorrect because it ends the clause with a preposition, which one generally should try to avoid doing when using standard written English.

34. **Correct Answer**: NO CHANGE

Explanation: "Decade" means period of ten consecutive years, so it is redundant to repeat this information. Thus, "decades and tens of years" is redundant. "Tens of years" is not as succinct as "decades," so it too is incorrect. "A ton" is too colloquial to be accepted in formal writing.

35. **Correct Answer**: an economic recession in England prevented continued construction on the tunnel

Explanation: The correct answer uses active voice, and the subject and verb are clear. The other choices are unclear, use passive voice, or are grammatically incorrect.

36. **Correct Answer**: I love cleaning.

Explanation: The word "cleaning" functions as a gerund in this sentence, so it can be treated like a noun. It is the predicate nominative of the verb "love."
"I love (blank)."
"I love cleaning." - The predicate nominative is a gerund.
"I love paper." - The predicate nominative is a noun.
"I hate reading." - The predicate nominative is a gerund.
"I hate food." - The predicate nominative is a noun.
It is grammatically correct to write, "I loved cleaning." However, the author uses the present tense in the rest of the paragraph, so the past tense does not fit here.

37. **Correct Answer**: nor

Explanation: Because the sentence uses the negative "neither," the negative "nor" should be used instead of "or," as "neither" matches with "nor," and "either" matches with "or."

38. **Correct Answer**: and I

Explanation: The comma usage is correct but "me" must be changed to "I" in order for the sentence to be grammatically correct. A good way to break this down is to use just the last two nouns to see what sounds right ("Alex and me get together" vs. "Alex and I get together").

39. **Correct Answer**: certain:

Explanation: The "two things I knew for certain" implies a list of two things, which requires a colon to separate the first clause from the subsequent list.

40. **Correct Answer**: sky, which was black and stormy,

Explanation: The correct answer uses a pair of commas to offset the unnecessary clause "which was black and stormy" from the main sentence. Using fewer or more commas than this is incorrect.
Remember: to test whether a clause is necessary or not, read the sentence without the clause to see if it is still a complete sentence.

41. **Correct Answer**: forget than

Explanation: There is no need for a comma because "than to hold grudges" is not a full sentence. Also, "than" is the correct word because you are making a comparision. "Then" is an adverb used to situate actions in time.

42. **Correct Answer**: NO CHANGE

Explanation: The sentence is correct as written. If the abbreviation "a.m." or "p.m." falls at the end of the sentence, an additional period is not necessary, but if it comes at the end of a dependent clause or a phrase that would otherwise end in a comma, the comma is required in addition to the period on the abbreviation. Because the sentence joins two complete sentences with a conjunction ("but"), the comma is required.

43. **Correct Answer**: All of these answers

Explanation: Prepositional phrases typically follow the structure "Preposition + Optional Modifiers (adjectives/adverbs) + Noun/Pronoun/Gerund."
This means that they are introduced by prepositions. "From," "through," and "outside" are all prepositions. Within the sentence, each introduces a prepositional phrase following the pattern ("from" + "the north," "through" + "the woods," "outside" + "the tent"). Thus, all of the answers are correct.

44. **Correct Answer**: NO CHANGE

Explanation: "Of" is the correct preposition here.

45. **Correct Answer**: The dog went to its doghouse and proceeded to bury all of its belongings.

Explanation: "While the apostrophe does mark possession in a phrase like "Tony's dog," the possessive form of the pronoun "it" is "its", without an apostrophe. "It's" is the contracted form of the phrase "it is", in which the apostrophe stands in for the missing "i" in "is".

46. **Correct Answer**: NO CHANGE

Explanation: The stable belongs to just one family. The possessive form of the singular word "family" is "family's."

47. **Correct Answer**: Did someone in here shout "Fire!"?

Explanation: Because the word "Fire" was shouted by someone, it requires an exclamation mark, and that exclamation mark should go inside the quotation marks, but since someone is asking if the word was shouted, the entire sentence is a question and should be marked with a question mark at the end. The entire sentence itself is not an exclamation, though, so ending the main sentence with an exclamation mark or the combination of a question mark and an exclamation mark would not be appropriate.

48. **Correct Answer**: Weighing more than 15,000 tons each, massive tunnel boring machines were used to dig the tunnel.

Explanation: This is an example of a misplaced modifier. When "workers" immediately follows the introductory clause "Weighing more than 15,000 tons each," the sentence actually implies that it is the workers rather than the machines that weigh 15,000 tons each. To prevent misplaced modifiers, keep the item being modified (in this case, the machines) as close to the modifier (in this case,
"Weighing more than 15,000 tons each") as possible. In the correct choice, "massive tunnel boring machines" follows the introductory clause; thus, the modifier correctly modifies the machines rather than the workers.

49. **Correct Answer**: to knit, sew, and create costumes

Explanation: This list is lacking proper parallelism. The activities in the sentence's list can all be infinitives (like "to knit") or gerunds (like "creating"), but not a mixture of the two. The correct answer choice fixes the sentence's error by changing all of the listed activities to infinitives.

50. **Correct Answer**: A two-thirds majority passed the new law.

Explanation: In passive voice, the object is acted upon ("The new law was passed"). In active voice, the subject performs an action ("A two-thirds majority passed"). Passive voice typically uses "to be" helping verbs (in this case, "was"). Thus, in order to rewrite the sentence in active voice, it is important to ensure that the subject performs an action and to eliminate "to be" helping verbs, but there is no need to eliminate the past tense. In fact, eliminating the past tense alters the timeline of the action, and is therefore wrong. "The new law passed by a two-thirds majority" changes the subject of the sentence from "a two-thirds majority" to "the new law," which should be the object of the action, so this sentence is not the BEST choice.

Practice Test 2: Math section

1. Which of the following is equal to $\sqrt{75}$?

- $5\sqrt{3}$
- 9
- $3\sqrt{5}$
- $7.5\sqrt{10}$

2. If 80% of a number is 240, what is 125% of the number?

- 375
- 200

- 325
- 250
- 300

3. 76 eleventh-grade students turned in term papers on the United States Constitution. 3 students failed, 26 students received C's, 31 students received B's. The remaining students earned A's on their papers.

What percentage of students earned A's on their paper? (Round to the nearest percent.)

- 10%
- 25%
- 50%
- 21%
- 16%

4. Place the following numbers in order from smallest to greatest:

5.13, 5.11, 5.131, 5.111, 5.115

- 5.111, 5.115, 5.11, 5.13, 5.131
- 5.13, 5.111, 5.115, 5.11, 5.131
- 5.11, 5.111, 5.115, 5.13, 5.131
- 5.13, 5.131, 5.115, 5.111, 5.11
- 5.13, 5.115, 5.111, 5.11, 5.131

5. If there are 75 calories in a 6 oz glass of juice, how many calories will there be in an 8 oz glass?

- 100 calories
- 225 calories
- 200 calories
- 150 calories
- 120 calories

6. Two angles are supplementary and have a ratio of 1:4. What is the size of the smaller angle?

- 144°
- 18°
- 72°
- 36°
- 45°

7. Points A, B, and C are collinear (they lie along the same line).
$\angle ACD = 90°$, $\angle CAD = 30°$, $\angle CBD = 60°$, $\overline{AD} = 4$

80

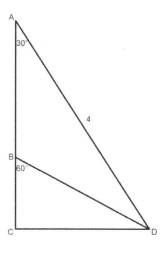

Find the length of segment $\overline{BD}$.

○ $\dfrac{4\sqrt{3}}{3}$

○ $\dfrac{\sqrt{3}}{2}$

○ $2\sqrt{3}$

○ $\dfrac{2\sqrt{3}}{3}$

○ 2

8. Points A, B, and C are collinear (they lie along the same line). The measure of angle CAD is 30°. The measure of angle CBD is 60°. The length of segment $\overline{AD}$ is 4.

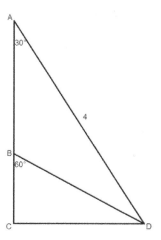

Find the measure of ∠ADB.

- ○ 45°
- ○ 60°
- ○ 30°
- ○ 15°
- ○ 90°

9. All segments of the polygon meet at right angles (90 degrees). The length of segment $\overline{AB}$ is 10. The length of segment $\overline{BC}$ is 8. The length of segment $\overline{DE}$ is 3. The length of segment $\overline{GH}$ is 2.

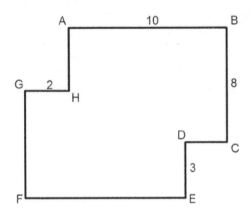

Find the perimeter of the polygon.

- ○ 48
- ○ 40
- ○ 46
- ○ 42
- ○ 44

10. A quadrilateral ABCD has diagonals that are perpendicular bisectors of one another. Which of the following classifications must apply to quadrilateral ABCD?

I. parallelogram
II. rhombus
III. square

- ○ I, II, and III
- ○ I and II only
- ○ II and III only
- ○ I and III only

11. Sides AB and AC in this triangle are equal. What is the measure of ∠A?

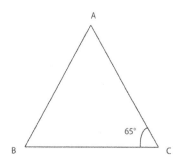

○ 40°
○ 180°
○ 130°
○ 65°
○ 50°

12. The radius of the circle above is 4 and ∠A = 45°. What is the area of the shaded section of the circle?

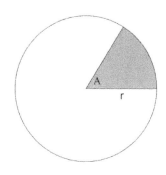

○ 8π
○ 2π
○ 16π
○ π
○ 4π

13. Two legs of a right triangle measure 3 and 4, respectively. What is the area of the circle that circumscribes the triangle?

○ 5π
○ 12.5π
○ 6π
○ 6.25π
○ 25π

14. A circle is inscribed in a square whose side is 6 in. What is the difference in area between the square and the circle, rounded to the nearest square inch?

○ $8\ in^2$
○ $12\ in^2$
○ $14\ in^2$
○ $11\ in^2$
○ $4\ in^2$

15. A thermometer reads an average of 47.5°F on a Sunday, rises 2.9 degrees on Monday, and drops 1.7 degrees on Tuesday. What is the average reading of the thermometer on Tuesday?

○   48.7°F
○   45.8°F
○   44.6°F
○   50.4°F
○   49.2°F

16. Find the arithmetic mean of the following set of data:

{1,2,3,4,6,8}

○   4
○   5
○   3
○   8
○   6

17. Jameson received four grades on his algebra tests, which brought his average to an 88. What grade would he have to make on his final test in order to bring his average up to a 90?

○   100
○   96
○   97
○   99
○   98

18. If the median of the set of numbers is 54 and the mean is 56, which of the following could be the values of x and y?

43, 83, 54, 35, 77, x, y

○   65 and 72
○   37 and 42
○   41 and 59
○   56 and 80
○   21 and 52

19. A bag contains 3 green marbles, 5 red marbles, and 9 blue marbles.

84

What is the probability of drawing a red marble?

- ○ 5
- ○ $\dfrac{5}{17}$
- ○ $\dfrac{5}{9}$
- ○ $\dfrac{5}{12}$
- ○ $\dfrac{5}{3}$

20. What is the probability of getting a sum of four when rolling two six-sided dice?

- ○ $\dfrac{1}{12}$
- ○ $\dfrac{7}{36}$
- ○ $\dfrac{1}{6}$
- ○ $\dfrac{5}{6}$
- ○ $\dfrac{1}{9}$

21. What is the volume of a sphere with a diameter of 6 in?

- ○ $216\pi\ in^3$
- ○ $72\pi\ in^3$
- ○ $36\pi\ in^3$
- ○ $108\pi\ in^3$
- ○ $288\pi\ in^3$

22. The radius of a sphere is 6. What is the approximate volume of this sphere?

- ○ 138π
- ○ 516π
- ○ 288π
- ○ 20π
- ○ 300π

23. What is the surface area of a square pyramid with a height of 12 in and a base side length of 10 in?

- 150 in^2
- 360 in^2
- 420 in^2
- 100 in^2
- 260 in^2

24. What line is parallel to 5x+3y = 8, and passes through the point (6,−4)?

- $y = \dfrac{1}{3}x - 3$

- $y = \dfrac{-5}{3}x + 6$

- $y = \dfrac{3}{2}x - 4$

- $y = \dfrac{-2}{3}x + 5$

- $y = \dfrac{3}{5}x - 2$

25. Which pair of linear equations represent parallel lines?

- y = 2x − 4
  y = 2x + 5

- y = x + 2
  y = −x + 2

- y = 2x + 4
  y = x + 4

- y = −x + 4
  y = x + 6

- y = x − 5
  y = 3x + 5

26. Which line below is perpendicular to 5x + 6y = 18?

- $y = \dfrac{5}{6}x + 2$

- $y = -\dfrac{6}{5}x + 8$

- $y = -.\dfrac{5}{6}x + \dfrac{6}{5}$

- $y = \dfrac{5}{6}x + \dfrac{6}{5}$
- $y = \dfrac{6}{5}x + 3$

27. Which of the following sets of coordinates are on the line y.= 3x − 4?

- (3,4)
- (1,2)
- (2,2)
- (1,5)
- (2,−2)

28. What is the slope of a line running through points (7,3) and (8,−4)?

- 7

- $-\dfrac{1}{7}$

- −7

- $\dfrac{7}{3}$

- 1

29. Which of the following equations does NOT represent a line?

- $x^2 + y = 10$
- $x + y = 10$
- $x - y = 10$
- $x = 10$
- $5y = 10$

30. In the standard (x,y) coordinate plane, what is the perimeter of a triangle with vertices at (0,1), (4,7) and (8,1).

- $13 + 4\sqrt{13}$
- $8 + 4\sqrt{52}$
- $2\sqrt{13} + 8$
- $8 + 4\sqrt{13}$
- $8 + \sqrt{52}$

31. At what point do the lines $y = \dfrac{1}{4}x + 7$ and $y = 4x + 7$ intersect?

- (0,−7)

- They do not intersect
- (7,0)
- (0,0)
- (0,7)

32. Solve $|z + 5| > 2$

- $z > 5$
- $2 < z < 5$
- $z < 2$
- $z > -3$ or $z < -7$
- $-7 < z < -3$

33. Solve $|z - 3| \leq 5$

- All real numbers
- $-2 \leq z \leq 8$
- $z \leq 8$
- $-2 \geq z$
- No solutions

34. Which of the following is equivalent to $2x^2 (xy^2 + 5x^2 y^2)$?

- $2x^3 y^2 + x^4 y^2$
- $2xy^2 + x^4 y^2$
- $2x^3 y^2 + 10x^4 y$
- $x^3 y^2 + 10x^4 y^2$
- $2x^3 y^2 + 10x^4 y^2$

35. What value of x and y solve the following system of equations?

$3x + 3y = 15$
$y - x = 3$

- $x = 4, y = 1$
- $x = 2, y = 5$
- $x = 1, y = 4$
- $x = 2, y = 3$
- $x = 1, y = 1$

36. If $x^2 = 25$ and $y^2 = 81$, what is the greatest value that $(x - y)^2$ can have?

- 16
- 100
- 25

○ 196
○ 81

37. Simplify: $\dfrac{x^{-2}y^5z^{-4}}{x^4y^3}$

○ $\dfrac{x^6y^2}{z^4}$

○ $\dfrac{y^8}{x^6z^4}$

○ $\dfrac{y^2z^4}{x^2}$

○ $\dfrac{y^2}{x^2z^4}$

○ $\dfrac{y^2}{x^6z^4}$

38. For all x, $(5x + 2)^2$ = ?

○ $25x^2 + 20x + 4$
○ $25x^2 + 4$
○ $10x^2 + 4$
○ $10x + 4$
○ $25x^2 + 10x + 4$

39. What value of x satisfies the equation log_x 64 = 2 ?

○ 8
○ 6
○ 10
○ 2
○ 4

40. If a = 2 and b = 4, what is $-4(ab)^3 + (3a - 2b)$?

○ −2046
○ 2046
○ −2050
○ 2050
○ −32,770

41. *f* pigeons land on a telephone wire. Then, g + 2 pigeons fly away. Find an expression for the number of pigeons remaining.

○ $f - g - 2$

- $f + g + 2$
- $2(f - g)$
- $f - g + 2$
- $2(f + g)$

42. If $f(x) = 4x^2 + 3x + 2$ and $g(x) = x + 7$, what is $f(g(x))$?

- $4x^2 + 3x + 72$
- $4x^2 + 17x + 219$
- $4x^2 + 3x + 219$
- $4x^2 + 59x + 219$
- $4x^2 + 17x + 72$

43. If $f(x) = x^2 + 3$, then $f(x + h) = ?$

- $x^2 + 3 + h$
- $x^2 + h^2$
- $x^2 + 2xh + h^2 + 3$
- $x^2 + 2xh + h^2$
- $x^2 + h^2 + 3$

44. If $f(6) = 7$ and $f(10) = 17$, which of the following could represent $f(x)$?

- $1.5x - 2$
- $2.5x - 8$
- $3x - 1$
- $x + 4$
- $2x + 5$

45.

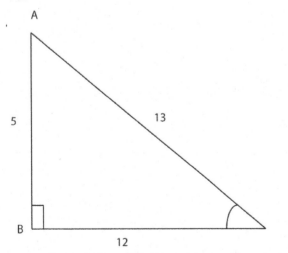

What is the sine of ∠ACB?

- $\dfrac{12}{5}$

○ $\frac{5}{13}$

○ $\frac{12}{13}$

○ $\frac{5}{12}$

○ 60º

Answer sheet with explanation

1. **Correct Answer**: $5\sqrt{3}$

Explanation: $\sqrt{75}$ can be broken down to $\sqrt{25} * \sqrt{3}$. Which simplifies to $5\sqrt{3}$.

2. **Correct Answer**: 375

Explanation: Since 80% of the number is 240, the number is $\frac{240}{80}$ which equals 300. Then calculate 125% of 300: 1.25 × 300 = 375.

3. **Correct Answer**: 21%

Explanation: Subtract 3, 26, and 31 from 76 to figure out how many students got A's (16). $\frac{16}{76}$ x 100

4. **Correct Answer**: 5.11, 5.111, 5.115, 5.13, 5.131

Explanation: When comparing decimals, move left to right, comparing the size of the tenths, then the hundredths, then the thousandths, etc....

5. **Correct Answer**: 100 calories

Explanation: We set up a proportion:
$\frac{x}{75} = \frac{8}{6}$ where x = calories.
We cross multiply to get 6x = 600, so there will be 100 calories in 8 oz of juice.

6. **Correct Answer**: 36º

Explanation: Since the angles are supplementary, their sum is 180 degrees. Because they are in a ratio of 1:4, the following expression could be written:

x + 4x = 180
5x = 180
x = 36°

7. **Correct Answer**: $\frac{4\sqrt{3}}{3}$

Explanation: The length of segment $\overline{BD}$ is $\frac{4\sqrt{3}}{3}$
Note that triangles ACD and BCD are both special, 30-60-90 right triangles. Looking specifically at triangle ACD, because we know that segment $\overline{AD}$ has a length of 4, we can determine that the length of segment $\overline{CD}$ is 2 using what we know about special right triangles. Then, looking at triangle BCD now, we can use the same rules to determine that segment $\overline{BD}$ has a length of $\frac{4}{\sqrt{3}}$ which simplifies to $\frac{4\sqrt{3}}{3}$

8. **Correct Answer**: 30°

Explanation: The measure of ∠ADB is 30°. Since A, B, and C are collinear, and the measure of ∠CBD is 60°, we know that the measure of ∠ABD is 120°.
Because the measures of the three angles in a triangle must add up to 180°, and two of the angles in triangle ABD are 30° and 120°, the third angle, ∠ADB, is 30°.

9. **Correct Answer**: 46

Explanation: The perimeter of the polygon is 46. Think of this polygon as a rectangle with two of its corners "flipped" inwards. This "flipping" changes the area of the rectangle, but not its perimeter; therefore, the top and bottom sides of the original rectangle would be 12 units long (10 + 2 = 12). The left and right sides would be 11 units long (8 + 3 = 11). Adding all four sides, we find that the perimeter of the rectangle (and therefore, of this polygon) is 46.

10. **Correct Answer**: I and II only

Explanation: If the diagonals of a quadrilateral are perpendicular bisectors of one another, then the quadrilateral must be a rhombus, but not necessarily a square. Since all rhombi are also parallelograms, quadrilateral ABCD must be both a rhombus and parallelogram.

11. **Correct Answer**: 50°

Explanation: This triangle has an angle of 65°. We also know it has another angle of 65° at ∠ABC because the two sides are equal. Adding those two angles together gives us 130° total. Since a triangle has 180° total, we subtract 130 from 180 and get 50.

12. **Correct Answer**: 2π

Explanation:
Area of Circle = $\pi r^2 = \pi 4^2 = 16\pi$

Total degrees in a circle = 360
Therefore 45 degree slice = 45/360 fraction of circle = 1/8
Shaded Area = 1/8 * Total Area = 1/8 * 16π = 2π

13. **Correct Answer**: $6.25\,\pi$

Explanation: For the circle to contain all 3 vertices, the hypotenuse must be the diameter of the circle. The hypotenuse, and therefore the diameter, is 5, since this must be a 3-4-5 right triangle.
The equation for the area of a circle is A = πr^2
A = $\pi(5/2)^2$ = 6.25π

14. **Correct Answer**: $8\ in^2$

Explanation: The circle is inscribed in a square when it is drawn within the square so as to touch in as many places as possible. This means that the side of the square is the same as the diameter of the circle.
Let π = 3.14

A_{square} = s² = (6)² = 36in²

A_{circle} = πr^2 = 3.14 · 3² =3.14· 9 = 28.26 in²

So the approximate difference is in area $8\ in^2$

15. **Correct Answer**: 48.7°F

Explanation: Use 47.5 as a baseline value to add and subtract the subsequent drops on Monday and Tuesday. Thus, 47.5 + 2.9 = 50.4 (Monday);
50.4 - 1.7 = 48.7 (Tuesday).

16. **Correct Answer**: 4

Explanation: The total sum of the elements of the set is 24. There are 6 terms in the set.
24/6 = 4

17. **Correct Answer**: 98

Explanation: To start, we have to understand the concept behind averages. To average something, take all your numbers, add them together and then divide by the total amount of numbers. Also, the definition of an average is a quantity intermediate to a set of quantities, or in other words, the exact middle.
In this particular problem, we know that the average of the first four tests is an 88, which means that the summation of the first four tests divided by 4 must equal 88. We can extrapolate from the definition of an average that the first four tests can all be estimated at 88. When adding in the fifth test, we must then account for 5 tests as opposed to 4. We can set up and solve the formula for the fifth test's grade as such:
(x = fifth test)

$$\frac{88+88+88+88+x}{5} = 90$$

Multiply both sides by 5.

$352 + x = 450$

$x = 98$

Jameson must score a 98 on his last test to bring his average up to a 90.

18. **Correct Answer**: 41 and 59

Explanation: The median is the numerical value separating the higher half of the data sample from the lower half. Rearrange the data set by increasing value:
35,43, 54, 77,83
In order for 54 to remain the median, either:
1. One of the variables must be greater than 54 and the other must be less than 54.
or
2. Both variables must be equal to 54.
This eliminates all answer choices except 41 and 59. The mean of the data set including these two values is 56.

19. **Correct Answer**: $\frac{5}{17}$

Explanation: The probability of drawing a red marble is $\frac{5}{17}$
The total number of marbles (3 + 5 + 9) is 17, so there are 17 possible outcomes. 5 of these possible outcomes are red marbles, so the probability of a red marble out of any marble is $\frac{5}{17}$

20. **Correct Answer**: $\frac{1}{12}$

Explanation: The sample space for rolling two six-sided dice 36, since each die has 6 sides.
6 * 6 = 36
There are three ways to roll a four.
1 and 3
2 and 2
3 and 1
The probability of rolling a four is given by the number of outcomes that produce a four divided by the total number of outcomes.

$$\frac{3 \; outcomes \; to \; get \; four}{36 \; outcomes \; total} = \frac{1}{12}$$

21. **Correct Answer**: $36\pi \; in^3$

Explanation: The formula for the volume of a sphere is:

$$V = \frac{4}{3}\pi r^3$$

where r = radius. The diameter is 6 in, so the radius will be 3 in.

22. **Correct Answer**: 288π

Explanation:

Volume = $\frac{4}{3}\pi r^3$

$V = \frac{4}{3}\pi(6)^3$

$V = \frac{4}{3}\pi(216)$

$V = 288\pi$

23. **Correct Answer**: $360\ in^2$

Explanation: The surface area of a square pyramid can be broken into the area of the square base and the areas of the four triangular sides. The area of a square is given by:
A = s² = $100\ in^2$
The area of a triangle is:
$A = \frac{1}{2}bh$
The given height of 12 in is from the vertex to the center of the base. We need to calculate the slant height of the triangular face by using the Pythagorean Theorem:
SH² = H² + B²
where H = 12 and B = 5 (half the base side) resulting in a slant height of 13 in.
So, the area of the triangle is:
$A = \frac{1}{2}bh = \frac{1}{2} \cdot 10 \cdot 13 = 65\ in^2$
There are four triangular sides totaling $260\ in^2$ for the sides.
The total surface area is thus $360\ in^2$, including all four sides and the base.

24. **Correct Answer**: y = $\frac{-5}{3}$ x + 6

Explanation: Converting the given line to slope-intercept form we get the following equation:
$y = \frac{-5}{3}x + \frac{8}{3}$
For parallel lines, the slopes must be equal, so the slope of the new line must also be $\frac{-5}{3}$. We can plug the new slope and the given point into the slope-intercept form to solve for the y-intercept of the new line.
y = mx + b

$-4 = \dfrac{-5}{3}(6) + b$

$-4 = -10 + b$

$b = 6$

Use the y-intercept in the slope-intercept equation to find the final answer.

$y = \dfrac{-5}{3}x + 6$

25. **Correct Answer**: $y = 2x - 4$ $y = 2x + 5$

Explanation: Parallel lines will always have equal slopes. The slope can be found quickly by observing the equation in slope-intercept form and seeing which number falls in the "m" spot in the linear equation ($y = mx + b$), we are looking for an answer choice in which both equations have the same m value. Both lines in the correct answer have a slope of 2, therefore they are parallel.

26. **Correct Answer**: $y = \dfrac{6}{5}x + 3$

Explanation: The definition of a perpendicular line is one that has a negative, reciprocal slope to another.

For this particular problem, we must first manipulate our initial equation into a more easily recognizable and useful form: slope-intercept form or $y = mx + b$.

$5x + 6y = 18$

$6y = -5x + 18$

$y = \dfrac{5}{6}x + 6$

According to our $y = mx + b$ formula, our slope for the original line is $-\dfrac{5}{6}$. We are looking for an answer that has a perpendicular slope, or an opposite reciprocal. The opposite reciprocal of $-\dfrac{5}{6}$ is $\dfrac{6}{5}$. Flip the original and multiply it by -1.

Our answer will have a slope of $\dfrac{6}{5}$. Search the answer choices for $\dfrac{6}{5}$ in the m position of the $y = mx + b$ equation.

$y = \dfrac{6}{5}x + 3$ is our answer.

(As an aside, the negative reciprocal of 4 is $-\dfrac{1}{4}$. Place the whole number over one and then flip/negate. This does not apply to the above problem, but should be understood to tackle certain permutations of this problem type where the original slope is an integer.)

27. **Correct Answer**: (2,2)

Explanation: (2, 2) when plugged in for y and x make the linear equation true, therefore those coordinates fall on that line.

y = 3x - 4
2 = 3(2) - 4
2 = 6 - 4
2 = 2

Because this equation is true, the point must lie on the line. The other given answer choices do not result in true equalities.

28. **Correct Answer**: -7

Explanation: The slope is equal to the difference between the y-coordinates divided by the difference between the x-coordinates.

$$m = \frac{y_2 - y_1}{x_2 - x_1}$$

Use the give points in this formula to calculate the slope.

$$m = \frac{3-(-4)}{7-8} = \frac{7}{-1} = -7$$

29. **Correct Answer**: x² + y = 10

Explanation: The answer is x² +y = 10.
A line can only be represented in the form x = z or y = mx + b, for appropriate constants z, m, and b. A graph must have an equation that can be put into one of these forms to be a line. x² + y = 10 represents a parabola, not a line. Lines will never contain an x² term.

30. **Correct Answer**: $8 + 4\sqrt{13}$

Explanation: This problem is a combination of two mathematical principles: the distance formula between two points, and the reduction of radicals.
To begin this problem, we must find the lengths of all sides of the triangle. Because we have the coordinates of the end points of each side, we can apply the distance formula.
$\sqrt{(x_2 - x_1)^2 + (y_2 - y_1)^2}$ = distance
between the two points $(x_1 \cdot y_1)$ and $(x_2 \cdot y_2)$
The application of this formula by writing out all the symbols and inserting the points and perhaps using a calculator is cumbersome and can be time consuming. There is a faster application of this formula in a geometric sense. Follow the steps below to give this process a try. This should be repeated for each distance you are trying to find and, in our case, it is three different distances.
1) Draw a right triangle with one leg horizontal and one vertical.
2) For the horizontal leg, find the distance between the x coordinates of the two chosen points and write down that distance: $(x_2 - x_1)$.
3) Repeat for the vertical leg substituting the y coordinates: $(y_2 - y_1)$
4) Apply the Pythagorean Theorem, where a and b are the horizontal and vertical leg in no particular order.
5 Solve for c.
c is the length of one of the sides of your triangle in which you wish to find the perimeter. If the formula is faster for you, use it. If the geometric method is faster and easier to visualize, use that one instead.

After applying the formula to all three legs, you'll find that you have the lengths, $\sqrt{52}$, $\sqrt{52}$ and 8. Once you add them together to find the perimeter (the perimeter of a triangle is all sides added together), you have the value $8 + 2\sqrt{52}$. Unfortunately, you won't find the answer as you still need to simplify the radical.

To go about reducing the radical you will need to break down 52 into its prime factors: 13, 2, and 2. (As an aside, any even number can be checked for prime factors by dividing it by two until it is no longer even.) Since there are two 2's under the radical, we can rewrite the radical as $\sqrt{2 \cdot 2 \cdot 13}$ or $\sqrt{2 \cdot 2} \cdot \sqrt{13}$ Since $\sqrt{4} = 2$ we can reduce $\sqrt{52}$ to $2\sqrt{13}$.

Therefore, $8 + 2\sqrt{52}$ can be rewritten $8 + 2(2)\sqrt{13}$ or $8 + 4\sqrt{13}$, which is our perimeter.

31. Correct Answer: (0,7)

Explanation: Short way:

The lines intersect somewhere because they have different slopes. Because they have the same y-intercept, they must intersect at that point.

Long way using substitution:

$y = \frac{1}{4}x + 7$

$y - 7 = \frac{1}{4}x$

$x = 4y - 28$

Plug this into $y = -4x + 7$

$y = -4(4y - 28) + 7$

$y = -16y + 112 + 7$

$17y = 119$

$y = 7$

Find x

$x = 4(7) - 28 = 0$

32. Correct Answer: z > −3 or z < − 7

Explanation: Absolute value problems are broken into two inequalities: $z + 5 > 2$ and $z + 5 < -2$. Each inequality is solved separately to get $z > -3$ and $z < -7$. Graphing each inequality shows that the correct answer is $z > -3$ or $z < -7$.

33. Correct Answer: −2 ≤ z ≤ 8

Explanation: Absolute value is the distance from the origin and is always positive.
So, we need to solve $z - 3 \leq 5$ and $z - 3 \geq -5$ which becomes a bounded solution.
Adding 3 to both sides of the inequality gives $z \leq 8$ and $z \geq -2$ or in simplified form $-2 \leq z \leq 8$

34. **Correct Answer**: 2x³ y² + 10x^4y²

Explanation: To determine the answer, 2x2 must be distributed, (2x² * xy²) + (2x² * 5x²y²). After multiplying the terms, the expression simplifies to 2x³y² + 10x^4y².

35. **Correct Answer**: x = 1, y = 4

Explanation: To solve the system of equations, 3x + 3y = 15 and y - x = 3, we must begin by inserting one equation into another. First notice that there are two variables and that we have two equations, therefore, we have enough equations to solve for both variables.
As an aside, for each variable, you need that many equations to solve for all variables.
We will insert the equations by substitution, which tends to be a more useful form of equation integration. As the y - x = 3 is the easier equation to solve for one variable, we'll start there. Solve for y.
y - x = 3 add x to both sides.
y = 3 +x
From here can insert this equation into all y's in our other equation and solve
3x + 3(3 + x) = 15) distribute
3x + 9 + 3x = 15 combine like terms
6x + 9 = 15 subtract 9 from both sides
6x = 15 – 9 divides by 6
x = $\frac{6}{6}$
x = 1
From here we reinsert this value into our y = 3 + x equation.
y = 3 +1
y = 4
Solution: x = 1, y = 4

36. **Correct Answer**: 196

Explanation: Solving for x yields -5 and 5. Solving for y yields -9 and 9.
The greatest difference between these two numbers is 14, and 14 squared is 196.

37. **Correct Answer**: $\frac{y^2}{x^6 z^4}$

Explanation: To tackle this problem we must understand the concept of exponents in fractions and how to cancel and move them.
To move any variable or number from the numerator to the denominator or vice versa, you must negate the exponent. i.e. x² in the numerator would become x^{-2} in the denominator. These two expressions are equivalent. You should strive to make all exponents positive initially before applying the next rule to simplify.
Cancelling variables with a similar base is an easy way to simplify.
Add or subtract the exponents depending on their relationship in a fraction.

Ex. $\frac{x}{x} = \frac{1}{1}$ or 1.

Ex. $\frac{x^2}{x} = x.$ → this can be more easily understood if you break down the x² · $\frac{(x \cdot x)}{x}$ which then can be moved around to form, $\frac{x}{x} \cdot$ x. After the $\frac{x}{x}$ cancels to form 1, we have 1 • x or just x. This can be applied for all numerical or abstract values of exponents for a given variable, such as x, y or z.

Knowing these rules, we can tackle the problem.

To begin we will pick a variable to start with, thereby breaking down the problem into three smaller chunks. First, we will start with the variable x. $\frac{x^{-2}}{x^4}$. Because the numerator has a negative exponent, we will move it down to the denominator: $\frac{1}{x^2 \cdot x^4}$. This simplifies to $\frac{1}{x^6}$ as multiplying any common variables with exponents is found by addition of the exponents atop the original variable. The x variable part of this problem is $\frac{1}{x^6}$.

We move to the y section of the problem: $\frac{y^5}{y^3}$. This is similar to our $\frac{x^2}{x}$ above, instead with larger numerical exponents.

$\frac{y \cdot y \cdot y \cdot y \cdot y}{y \cdot y \cdot y} = \frac{y \cdot y \cdot y}{y \cdot y \cdot y} \cdot (y \cdot y)$. The $\frac{y \cdot y \cdot y}{y \cdot y \cdot y}$ section cancels, leaving us with y · y or y².

Now to the z section. We simply have z^{-4} on top. Applying the first rule above, we just move it to the denominator with the switching of the sign. Our result is $\frac{1}{z^4}$.

Combining all the sections together we have $\frac{1}{x^6} \cdot$ y² $\cdot \frac{1}{z^4}$.

More beautifully written it looks like $\frac{y^2}{x^6 z^4}$.

38. **Correct Answer**: 25x² + 20x + 4

Explanation: (5x + 2)² is equivalent to (5x + 2)(5x + 2).
Using the FOIL method, you multiply the first number of each set 5x • 5x = 25x², multiply the outer numbers of each set 5x • 2 = 10x, multiply the inner numbers of each set 2 • 5x = 10x, and multiply outer numbers of each set 2 • 2 = 4.
Adding all these numbers together, you get 25x² + 10x + 10x + 4 = 25x² + 20x + 4.

39. **Correct Answer**: 8

Explanation: log_x 64 = 2 can by rewritten as x² = 64.
In this form the question becomes a simple exponent problem.
The answer is 8 because 8² = 64.

40. **Correct Answer**: −2050

Explanation:

-4(2 · 4)³ + (3 · 2 − 2 · 4)
-4(512) + (6 - 8)
-2048 - 2
-2050

41. **Correct Answer**: $f - g - 2$

Explanation: There are f - g - 2 pigeons remaining on the wire. We start with f pigeons, then subtract (g + 2) pigeons. f - (g + 2) = f - g - 2.

42. **Correct Answer**: $4x^2 + 59x + 219$

Explanation:
$4(x + 7)^2 + 3(x + 7) + 2$
$4(x^2 + 14x + 49) + 3x + 21 + 2$
$4x^2 + 56x + 196 + 3x + 23$
$4x^2 + 59x + 219$

43. **Correct Answer**: $x^2 + 2xh + h^2 + 3$

Explanation:
To find f(x + h) when f(x) = x² + 3, we substitute (x + h) for x in f(x).
Thus, f(x + h) = (x + h)² + 3.
We expand (x + h)² to x² + xh + xh + h².
We can combine like terms to get x² + 2xh + h².
We add 3 to this result to get our final answer.

44. **Correct Answer**: $2.5x - 8$

Explanation: The number in the parentheses is what goes into the function.
For the function f(x) = 2.5x - 8,
f(6) = 2.5(6) - 8 = 7 and
f(10) = 2.5(10) - 8 = 17

45. **Correct Answer**: $\dfrac{5}{13}$

Explanation: Sine can be found using the SOH CAH TOA method. For sine we do $\dfrac{opposite}{hypotenuse}$.

Practice Test 3: Reading section

Passage:

When we study law, we are not studying a mystery but a well-known profession. We are studying what we shall want in order to appear before judges, or to advise people in such a way as to keep them out of court. The reason why it is a profession, why people will pay lawyers to argue for them or to advise them, is that in societies like ours the command of the public force is intrusted to the judges in certain cases, and the whole power of the state will be put forth, if necessary, to carry out their judgments and decrees. People want to know under what circumstances and how far they will run the risk of coming against what is so much stronger than themselves, and hence it becomes a business to find out when this danger is to be feared. The object of our study, then, is prediction, the prediction of the incidence of the public force through the instrumentality of the courts.

The means of the study are a body of reports, of treatises, and of statutes, in this country and in England, extending back for six hundred years, and now increasing annually by hundreds. In these sibylline leaves are gathered the scattered prophecies of the past upon the cases in which the axe will fall. These are what properly have been called the oracles of the law. Far the most important and pretty nearly the whole meaning of every new effort of legal thought is to make these prophecies more precise, and to generalize them into a thoroughly connected system. The process is one, from a lawyer's statement of a case, eliminating as it does all the dramatic elements with which his client's story has clothed it, and retaining only the facts of legal import, up to the final analyses and abstract universals of theoretic jurisprudence. The reason why a lawyer does not mention that his client wore a white hat when he made a contract, while Mrs. Quickly would be sure to dwell upon it along with the parcel gilt goblet and the sea-coal fire, is that he foresees that the public force will act in the same way whatever his client had upon his head. It is to make the prophecies easier to be remembered and to be understood that the teachings of the decisions of the past are put into general propositions and gathered into textbooks, or that statutes are passed in a general form. The primary rights and duties with which jurisprudence busies itself again are nothing but prophecies. One of the many evil effects of the confusion between legal and moral ideas, about which I shall have something to say in a moment, is that theory is apt to get the cart before the horse, and consider the right or the duty as something existing apart from and independent of the consequences of its breach, to which certain sanctions are added afterward. But, as I shall try to show, a legal duty so called is nothing but a prediction that if a man does or omits certain things he will be made to suffer in this or that way by judgment of the court; and so of a legal right.

The number of our predictions when generalized and reduced to a system is not unmanageably large. They present themselves as a finite body of dogma which may be mastered within a reasonable time. It is a great mistake to be frightened by the ever-increasing number of reports. The reports of a given jurisdiction in the course of a generation take up pretty much the whole body of the law, and restate it from the present point of view. We could reconstruct the corpus from them if all that went before were burned.

Questions:

1. Which of the following most closely resembles proper theoretic jurisprudence as it is described by the author?

A. A philosopher starting with certain assumed truths and common sense principles, then combining them and teasing out their implications to deduce what must be done to resolve ethical dilemmas

B. A philosopher conducting thought experiments to test the soundness of a theory under extreme cases, documenting where the theory produced counterintuitive or paradoxical results

C. A biologist noticing trends in a set of collected data, accounting and controlling for extranious variables, and creating a general model that can be applied to other relevant instances

D. An anthropologist conducting interviews and listening to the oral traditions of several different cultures, then constructing a theory that describes the development of cultural values in human societies

E. A physicist working with mathematical models to construct a theory, then testing this theory by conducting experiments

2. With which of the following positions would the author of this passage most likely disagree?

A. Legal principles are mainly aids to help guess how a law case will turn out.

B. While one can never learn every fact of the law, such learning is unnecessary to mastering the law.

C. In practicing law, one can only make predictions on how a particular case might turn out, and never certain ones.

D. There is nothing irrelevant to the practice of law.

E. While there may be a relationship between morality and law, the law is not simply a codification and enforcement of ethical principles.

3. Which of the following views is most nearly opposed to the main thesis of the author?

A. The proper subject of the study of law itself, as opposed to individual laws, is to derrive and deduce legal principles from first principles.

B. The law considers no detail irrelevant, no piece of evidence too small, in making its decisions; the most weighty matters are sometimes decided on what seem to be the most trivial of details.

C. Nobody can escape the "long arm of the law," and all fear it; thus, they seek the advice of attornies and counselors to avoid crossing those well-defined lines that are poorly known to the layman in which the law must act.

D. The law is often obscure, and open to interpretation; thus, the best lawyer is the one who can work in these "penumbras of the law," fashioning the best interpretation of it in the open spaces between certain cases.

E. The past dictates the present, and what has come before what comes now—indeed, what is to come. Thus, the student of law who knows the greatest part of the body of past law will have the best chance of predicting the outcome of present and future cases.

4. Which of the following best captures the primary point of the final paragraph?

A. New cases merely rehash and go over old issues in ways an experienced practicioner will have seen before. As such, one need not study old decisions and principles, as newer ones present them in exactly the same way.
B. It is not necessary to learn every single court decision, statute, or legal determination that has been issued in the last 600 years, as the relevent issues are recapitulated and reinterpreted regularly.
C. As laws are valid only in particular jurisdictions, and legal principles are derrived from these laws, it therefore follows that legal principles are valid only in certain jurisdictions; thus, while the body of law worldwide might seem overwhelming, one need only learn the laws of the jurisdictions in which one practices, and likewise only the principles that can be deduced from them.
D. The body of law, in its statutes, principles, and decisions, is increasing at such a rate that anyone who would hope to master it must constantly "run to stay in place;" by the time a practicioner has digested some part of the legal corpus, new decisions and statutes have supplanted what was learned.
E. The body of law is ever-increasing, with courts adding to it by the moment; as such, it is impossible to ever truly learn the whole of the law in the course of a single lifetime.

Passage:

To present a general view of the Common Law, other tools are needed besides logic. It is something to show that the consistency of a system requires a particular result, but it is not all. The life of the law has not been logic: it has been experience. The felt necessities of the time, the prevalent moral and political theories, intuitions of public policy, avowed or unconscious, even the prejudices which judges share with their fellow-men, have had a good deal more to do than the syllogism in determining the rules by which men should be governed. The law embodies the story of a nation's development through many centuries, and it cannot be dealt with as if it contained only the axioms and corollaries of a book of mathematics. In order to know what it is, we must know what it has been, and what it tends to become. We must alternately consult history and existing theories of legislation. But the most difficult labor will be to understand the combination of the two into new products at every stage. The substance of the law at any given time pretty nearly corresponds, so far as it goes, with what is then understood to be convenient; but its form and machinery, and the degree to which it is able to work out desired results, depend very much upon its past.

In Massachusetts today, while, on the one hand, there are a great many rules which are quite sufficiently accounted for by their manifest good sense, on the other, there are some which can only be understood by reference to the infancy of procedure among the German tribes, or to the social condition of Rome under the Decemvirs.

I shall use the history of our law so far as it is necessary to explain a conception or to interpret a rule, but no further. In doing so there are two errors equally to be avoided both by writer and reader. One is that of supposing, because an idea seems very familiar and natural to us, that it has always been so. Many things which we take for granted have had to be laboriously fought out or thought out in past times. The other mistake is the opposite one of asking too much of history. We start with man full grown. It may be assumed that the earliest barbarian whose practices are to be considered, had a good many of the same feelings and passions as ourselves.

Questions:

5. Which of the following statements would the author of this passage be most likely to agree with?

    A. "Rights and responsibilities flow from past decisions and so count as legal, not just when they are explicit in these decisions but also when they follow from the principles of personal and political morality the explicit decisions presuppose by way of justification."

    B. "Justice is what the judge had for breakfast."

    C. "We must always stand by past decisions, and not disturb the undisturbed."

    D. "We must beware of the pitfall of antiquarianism, and must remember that for our purposes our only interest in the past is for the light it throws upon the present."

    E. "Law aims to lay principle over practice to show the best route to a better future, keeping the right faith with the past."

6. Which of the following statements would the author of the passage be most likely to disagree with most strongly?

    A. There is, strictly speaking, no law apart from society; what is found in the one is found in the other.

    B. The story of law is seen in its history, a history that includes the present day and even the future.

    C. Human nature does not change, but the circumstances in which men live do; thus, some laws of great antiquity ought to still be followed, but others have outlived their use.

    D. The law is itself lawful, and the one who understands its first principles can reason to its conclusions.

    E. In studying the paths of the law, we can discern certain principles that appear time and again, and, inasmuch as they are useful for the present, ought to learn them.

7. Each of the following can be inferred from the passage EXCEPT _____.

    A. laws generally reflect the societies in which they were enacted

    B. there are some contemporary laws based in ancient Roman law

    C. there is no role for systematic logic in the interpretation of laws

    D. human nature has generally been the same throughout history

    E. many laws of ancient origin that have little relevance to contemporary society were once relevant to an older social order

8. Which of the following best describes the purpose of the underlined paragraph in the passage?

A. A specific example used as evidence to bolster a premise in an earlier argument
B. A set of examples used to illustrate an assertion earlier in the passage
C. An example illustrating the effects of applying procedures advocated for earlier
D. A rhetorical contrast between good sense and adherance to ancient tradition
E. A contrast between two approaches to understanding a single body of law

Passage:

The first thought that men had concerning the heavenly bodies was an obvious one: they were lights. There was a greater light to rule the day, a lesser light to rule the night, and there were the stars also.

In those days there seemed an immense difference between the earth upon which men stood and the bright objects that shone down upon it from the heavens above. The earth seemed to be vast, dark, and motionless; the celestial lights seemed to be small, and moved and shone. The earth was then regarded as the fixed center of the universe, but the Copernican theory has since deprived it of this pride of place. Yet from another point of view, the new conception of its position involves a promotion, since the earth itself is now regarded as a heavenly body of the same order as some of those that shine down upon us. It is amongst them, and it too moves and shines—shines, as some of them do, by reflecting the light of the sun. Could we transport ourselves to a neighboring world, the earth would seem a star, not distinguishable in kind from the rest.

But as men realized this, they began to ask, "Since this world from a distant standpoint must appear as a star, would not a star, if we could get near enough to it, show itself also as a world? This world teems with life; above all, it is the home of human life. Men and women, gifted with feeling, intelligence, and character, look upward from its surface and watch the shining members of the heavenly host. Are none of these the home of beings gifted with like powers, who watch in their turn the movements of that shining point that is our world?"

This is the meaning of the controversy on the Plurality of Worlds which excited so much interest some sixty years ago, and has been with us more or less ever since. It is the desire to recognize the presence in the orbs around us of beings like ourselves, possessed of personality and intelligence, lodged in an organic body.

This is what is meant when we speak of a world being "inhabited." It would not, for example, at all content us if we could ascertain that Jupiter was covered by a shoreless ocean, rich in every variety of fish, or that the hard rocks of the Moon were delicately veiled by lichens. Just as no richness of vegetation and no fullness and complexity of animal life would justify an explorer in describing some land that he had discovered as being "inhabited" if no men were there, so we cannot rightly speak of any other world as being "inhabited" if it is not the home of intelligent life.

On the other hand, of necessity we are precluded from extending our inquiry to the case of disembodied intelligences, if such be conceived possible. All created existences must be conditioned, but if we have no knowledge of what those conditions may be, or means for attaining such knowledge, we cannot discuss them. Nothing can be affirmed, nothing denied, concerning the possibility of intelligences existing on the Moon or even in the Sun if we are unable to ascertain under what limitations those particular intelligences subsist.

The only beings, then, the presence of which would justify us in regarding another world as "inhabited" are such as would justify us in applying that term to a part of our own world. They must possess intelligence and consciousness on the one hand; on the other, they must likewise have corporeal form. True, the form might be imagined as different from that we possess, but, as with ourselves, the intelligent spirit must be lodged in and expressed by a living material body. Our inquiry is thus rendered a physical one; it is the necessities of the living body that must guide us in it; a world unsuited for living organisms is not, in the sense of this enquiry, a "habitable" world.

Questions:

9. Which of the following statements does the passage most strongly suggest that the author would agree with?

    A. Science could possibly discover the truth about anything that could possibly exist.
    B. The work of Copernicus was a necessary step for people to be able to think of other worlds as possibly inhabited.
    C. There are some worlds that are home to beings without bodies, even though we cannot study these beings.
    D. The controversy of the plurality of worlds is settled.
    E. Every star is a world like our own.

10. Which of the following CANNOT be inferred from the passage?

    A. No uninhabited world is the home of intelligent beings.
    B. Some uninhabited world could be the home of intelligent beings.
    C. Some inhabited world could be the home of non-intelligent beings.
    D. Some uninhabited world could be the home of non-intelligent beings.
    E. Every inhabited world is the home of intelligent beings.

11. Which of the following best describes the primary purpose of the underlined final sentence of the passage?

    A. A key assumption assumed by earlier arguments that, if true, would validate them
    B. An additional, secondary conclusion that can be derived from the primary conclusion of the passage
    C. The primary conclusion of the passage, supported by an earlier subordinate conclusion
    D. A question raised by the conclusion of the passage that will be investigated later
    E. An empirical observation that must guide the theoretical model under consideration

12. Which of the following best describes the tone of the first three paragraphs?

   A. Witty and ironic
   B. Objective and serious
   C. Formal and didactic
   D. Reflective and philosophical
   E. Elegiac and wistful

13. Which of the following most accurately describes the main idea of the passage?

   A. In order for a world to be considered inhabited, it must have intelligent life with material bodies.
   B. The inhabitants of other worlds could have very different bodies than those of humans.
   C. As science has progressed, people have wondered if there are other worlds that might be inhabited by creatures like ourselves.
   D. Advances in science have allowed us to contemplate whether other worlds are inhabited.
   E. The presence of non-intelligent life, like lichens or oysters, is not sufficient to make another world inhabited.

14. Which of the following best describes the structure of the passage?

   A. Giving the history of the development of a theory; mentioning a consequence of this development; describing necessary conditions for a state of affairs; drawing conclusions from these conditions
   B. Describing a scientific problem; laying out some possible solutions to that problem; describing a new theory that addresses some of the common problems in previous models; addressing the limits of how this new theory can be applied
   C. Explaining the history of a scientific discipline; making deductions from the progress of this discipline; describing sufficient conditions for further progress in a particular area; laying out avenues for future investigation
   D. Describing the results of empirical investigations; conducting a thought experiment based on these results; describing further observations that fit both the initial investigation and the thought experiment; creating a new theoretical model
   E. Describing the development of a theoretical model; explaining how this model influenced more recent observations; describing a new application for the kinds of observations influenced by this model; mentioning how a different model could also account for these observations

15. What is the primary purpose of the fourth paragraph?

   A. To introduce a premise that will be used to support a conclusion in the final paragraph
   B. To transition between the historical and metaphysical survey of the opening paragraphs and the logical arguments of the following ones

C. To provide an introduction and historical context for the controversy of the plurality of worlds
D. To reach a secondary conclusion important to the main argument of the overall passage
E. To present evidence that will be used to counter an opposing argument

Passage:

When we try to ascertain the motives which have led men to the investigation of philosophical questions, we find that, broadly speaking, they can be divided into two groups, often antagonistic, and leading to very divergent systems. These two groups of motives are, on the one hand, those derived from religion and ethics, and, on the other hand, those derived from science. Plato, Spinoza, and Hegel may be taken as typical of the philosophers whose interests are mainly religious and ethical, while Leibniz, Locke, and Hume may be taken as representatives of the scientific wing. In Aristotle, Descartes, Berkeley, and Kant we find both groups of motives strongly present.

Herbert Spencer, in whose honor we are assembled today, would naturally be classed among scientific philosophers; it was mainly from science that he drew his data, his formulation of problems, and his conception of method. But his strong religious sense is obvious in much of his writing, and his ethical preoccupations are what make him value the conception of evolution—that conception in which, as a whole generation has believed, science and morals are to be united in fruitful and indissoluble marriage.

It is my belief that the ethical and religious motives, in spite of the splendidly imaginative systems to which they have given rise, have been, on the whole, a hindrance to the progress of philosophy, and ought now to be consciously thrust aside by those who wish to discover philosophical truth. Science, originally, was entangled in similar motives, and was thereby hindered in its advances. It is, I maintain, from science, rather than from ethics and religion, that philosophy should draw its inspiration.

But there are two different ways in which a philosophy may seek to base itself upon science. It may emphasize the most general results of science, and seek to give even greater generality and unity to these results. Or it may study the methods of science, and seek to apply these methods, with the necessary adaptations, to its own peculiar province. Much philosophy inspired by science has gone astray through preoccupation with the results momentarily supposed to have been achieved. It is not results, but methods that can be transferred with profit from the sphere of the special sciences to the sphere of philosophy. What I wish to bring to your notice is the possibility and importance of applying to philosophical problems certain broad principles of method which have been found successful in the study of scientific questions.

The opposition between a philosophy guided by scientific method and a philosophy dominated by religious and ethical ideas may be illustrated by two notions which are very prevalent in the works of philosophers, namely the notion of the universe, and the notion of good and evil. A philosopher is expected to tell us something about the nature of the universe as a whole, and to give grounds for either optimism or pessimism. Both these expectations seem to me mistaken. I believe the conception of "the universe" to be, as its etymology indicates, a mere relic of pre-Copernican astronomy, and I believe the question of optimism and pessimism to be one which the philosopher will regard as outside his scope, except, possibly, to the extent of maintaining that it is insoluble.

Questions:

16. With which of these statements would the author of this argument be most likely to disagree?

    A. Scientific inquiry has flourished in Twentieth and Twenty First Centuries due to an increasing neglect of religious motivations.
    B. The monasteries of Medieval Europe were centers of scientific learning because of their ability to merge religious and scientific inquiry cohesively.
    C. None of these; the author would agree with all these statements.
    D. Organized religion has had a profoundly negative impact on the development of scientific thought and inquiry.
    E. Philosophers' motivations may be classed as either scientific or as religious and ethical, or as drawing from both areas.

17.

The author of this passage would argue that determining the nature of the universe is
_____.

    A. fundamental to the field
    B. impossible
    C. pointless
    D. suspicious
    E. highly important, but challenging

18. Which of the following philosophers would the author be most likely to agree with and sympathize with?

    A. Plato
    B. Descartes
    C. Hegel
    D. Hume
    E. Kant

19. Based on the passage, which of the following is true?

    A. Only scientific philosophers are expected to tell us something about the nature of the universe.

B. Scientific results are remarkably useful when applied to the sphere of philosophy.

C. Science has experienced the same sort of setbacks in recent years as religion has during the past.

D. While many believe that evolution represents a successful combination of science and ethics, the author would likely disagree with this view.

E. A number of philosophers cannot be classed as either being motivated by science or as being motivated by ethics and religion.

20. The author's attitude towards religion is primarily _____.

A. critical and intolerant
B. bellicose and frustrated
C. disparaging and mocking
D. apathetic and cautious
E. dismissive and haughty

21. The author of this essay would most likely describe the relationship between scientific philosophy and religious philosophy as _____.

A. Wanton and pointless
B. Supplementary and positive
C. Hostile and non-complementary
D. Puzzling and oppositional
E. Surprising and overwhelming

22. This essay could best be titled _____.

A. "On the Importance of Religious Philosophical Inquiry"
B. "On Results-Based and Method-Based Scientific Philosophical Inquiry"
C. "In Praise of Herbert Spencer"
D. "On the Positive Applications of Scientific Method to Philosophy"
E. "In Defense of Scientific Inquiry and Exploration"

23. What does the author believe has long hindered the progress of science?

A. The general disdain for scientific investigation among the general population
B. The overriding influence of religious institutions
C. The inattention to detail among leading scientific figures
D. Ignorance of the scientific method among leading scientific figures
E. Its entanglement with religious and ethical motivations

Passage:

The spectator who casts a mournful view over the ruins of ancient Rome, is tempted to accuse the memory of the Goths and Vandals, for the mischief which they had neither leisure, nor power, nor perhaps inclination, to perpetrate. The tempest of war might strike some lofty turrets to the ground; but the destruction which undermined the foundations of those massy fabrics was prosecuted, slowly and silently, during a period of ten centuries; and the motives of interest, that afterwards operated without shame or control, were severely checked by the taste and spirit of the emperor Majorian. The decay of the city had gradually impaired the value of the public works. The circus and theaters might still excite, but they seldom gratified, the desires of the people: the temples, which had escaped the zeal of the Christians, were no longer inhabited, either by gods or men; the diminished crowds of the Romans were lost in the immense space of their baths and porticos; and the stately libraries and halls of justice became useless to an indolent generation, whose repose was seldom disturbed, either by study or business. The monuments of consular, or Imperial, greatness were no longer revered, as the immortal glory of the capital: they were only esteemed as an inexhaustible mine of materials, cheaper, and more convenient than the distant quarry. Specious petitions were continually addressed to the easy magistrates of Rome, which stated the want of stones or bricks, for some necessary service: the fairest forms of architecture were rudely defaced, for the sake of some paltry, or pretended, repairs; and the degenerate Romans, who converted the spoil to their own emolument, demolished, with sacrilegious hands, the labors of their ancestors. Majorian, who had often sighed over the desolation of the city, applied a severe remedy to the growing evil.

He reserved to the prince and senate the sole cognizance of the extreme cases which might justify the destruction of an ancient edifice; imposed a fine of fifty pounds of gold (two thousand pounds sterling) on every magistrate who should presume to grant such illegal and scandalous license, and threatened to chastise the criminal obedience of their subordinate officers, by a severe whipping, and the amputation of both their hands. In the last instance, the legislator might seem to forget the proportion of guilt and punishment; but his zeal arose from a generous principle, and Majorian was anxious to protect the monuments of those ages, in which he would have desired and deserved to live. The emperor conceived that it was his interest to increase the number of his subjects; and that it was his duty to guard the purity of the marriage-bed: but the means which he employed to accomplish these salutary purposes are of an ambiguous, and perhaps exceptionable, kind. The pious maids, who consecrated their virginity to Christ, were restrained from taking the veil till they had reached their fortieth year. Widows under that age were compelled to form a second alliance within the term of five years, by the forfeiture of half their wealth to their nearest relations, or to the state. Unequal marriages were condemned or annulled. The punishment of confiscation and exile was deemed so inadequate to the guilt of adultery, that, if the criminal returned to Italy, he might, by the express declaration of Majorian, be slain with impunity.

Questions:

24. The way in which the author describes the barbarians is analogous to _____.

    A. a man talking about his brother
    B. a person in a debate reassessing a misconceived subject
    C. an apologist talking about a taboo topic

D. a doctor describing a malignant and highly feared illness
E. a professor talking about rudimentary facts in a room full of experts

25. The passage provides evidence to suggest that the author would be most likely to assent to which one of the following proposals?

    A. There should have been allowances made for adultery.
    B. Majorian was too harsh towards the magistrates.
    C. The Romans displayed values and principles when they chose to demolish older buildings and monuments
    D. Majorian should have been laxer in trying to increase the numbers of his citizens.
    E. People had no right to utilize the decaying buildings for building materials.

26. The argument made suggests that the author believes _____.

    A. The Roman civilization is comparable to more modern civilizations.
    B. The Vandals were equal to the Goths and the Romans in culpability.
    C. Great buildings go towards making and defining a great culture.
    D. The enforcement of repopulation was a mistake, as it detracted from the number of nuns.
    E. We can learn from Majorian's mistakes.

27. Which of the following statements, if shown to be true, would most detract from the author's conclusions about the destruction of buildings and monuments?

    A. The city's plumbing was in some ways better than that of the modern world during the years in question.
    B. The amount of people visiting the temples at the time was actually quite high.
    C. A poll of the city from the dates in question revealed the popular opinion to be that the most important buildings were in fact the temples, monuments, and consular buildings.
    D. During the period in question the quarries sold more stone than in the previous century.
    E. Several of the ministers for architecture had plans to reinvigorate the city.

28. The author most likely lists some of Majorian's population control methods primarily to _____.

    A. criticize the policy
    B. honor the decisiveness of such a controversial set of rules, which by modern methods would be considered extreme
    C. bring the subjects of religion and marriage into the argument
    D. show that Majorian was striving, beyond reasonable morals, to reinstate Rome's greatness
    E. describe at length the procedures used as an example

Passage:

Some twenty-one years ago I heard the first great anarchist speaker—the inimitable John Most. It seemed to me then, and for many years after, that the spoken word hurled forth among the masses with such wonderful eloquence, such enthusiasm and fire, could never be erased from the human mind and soul. How could any one of all the multitudes who flocked to Most's meetings escape his prophetic voice! Surely they had but to hear him to throw off their old beliefs, and see the truth and beauty of anarchism!

My one great longing then was to be able to speak with the tongue of John Most, that I, too, might thus reach the masses. Oh, for the naivety of youth's enthusiasm! It is the time when the hardest thing seems but child's play. It is the only period in life worthwhile. Alas! This period is but of short duration. Like spring, the Sturm und Drang period of the propagandist brings forth growth, frail and delicate, to be matured or killed according to its powers of resistance against a thousand vicissitudes.

My great faith in the wonder-worker, the spoken word, is no more. I have realized its inadequacy to awaken thought, or even emotion. Gradually, and with no small struggle against this realization, I came to see that oral propaganda is at best but a means of shaking people from their lethargy: it leaves no lasting impression. The very fact that most people attend meetings only if aroused by newspaper sensations, or because they expect to be amused, is proof that they really have no inner urge to learn.

It is altogether different with the written mode of human expression. No one, unless intensely interested in progressive ideas, will bother with serious books. That leads me to another discovery made after many years of public activity. It is this: all claims of education notwithstanding, the pupil will accept only that which his mind craves. Already this truth is recognized by most modern educators in relation to the immature mind. I think it is equally true regarding the adult. Anarchists or revolutionists can no more be made than musicians. All that can be done is to plant the seeds of thought. Whether something vital will develop depends largely on the fertility of the human soil, though the quality of the intellectual seed must not be overlooked.

In meetings the audience is distracted by a thousand non-essentials. The speaker, though ever so eloquent, cannot escape the restlessness of the crowd, with the inevitable result that he will fail to strike root. In all probability he will not even do justice to himself.

The relation between the writer and the reader is more intimate. True, books are only what we want them to be; rather, what we read into them. That we can do so demonstrates the importance of written as against oral expression. It is this certainty that has induced me to gather in one volume my ideas on various topics of individual and social importance. They represent the mental and soul struggles of twenty-one years—the conclusions derived after many changes and inner revisions.

Questions:

29. The author of this passage would be most likely to disagree with which of the following?

   A. An argument that youthful enthusiasm and certainty is often misplaced.
   B. A dissertation on the difficulties of impacting individuals through oration and spoken propaganda.
   C. An essay explaining the inherent value of the anarchist movement.
   D. A statement that the relationship between the reader and writer is as detached as the relationship between speaker and listener.
   E. A biographic exposition that praises the impact of John Most on the anarchist movement.

30. What does the author believe is the best-case scenario that can result from oral propaganda?

   A. The listener will be awoken from his or her apathy.
   B. The audience will be collectively inspired to act.
   C. The individual will be forced to reconsider his or her opinions and may even join the movement.
   D. None of these answers; the author believes that almost nothing good can come from oral propaganda to the extent that it is essentially pointless.
   E. The individual will seek to further advance his or her knowledge on the subject.

31. Which of these bests restates the meaning of the underlined sentence, "Like Spring, the STURM UND DRANG period of the propagandist brings forth growth, frail and delicate, to be matured or killed according to its powers of resistance against a thousand vicissitudes"?

   A. In the face of widespread criticism, the opinions of the propagandist are likely to be severely tested during the early periods of his or her activism; they require constant nurturing to preserve them.
   B. The propagandist is a weak and easily swayed individual who requires constant nurturing during the early periods of his or her life; otherwise he or she will quickly abandon the cause in favor of something more universally agreeable.
   C. During the early period of an activist's life his or her opinions usually become set in stone and are only subject to change if the resistance of the individual is too weak to resist the impositions and criticisms of others.
   D. The early period of an activist's life is crucial to the formation of his or her ideas; it is best that those ideas be heavily questioned by the individual in order to ensure they are what he or she truly believes.
   E. The turbulent and emotional young period of an activist's life changes how they approach their work; it can lead to a maturity or abandonment of values depending on the will of the individual to resist change or complete alteration.

32. This essay is most likely _____.

A. the conclusion to a piece about the author's changes from youthful optimism to mature realism
B. the conclusion to a piece about the value of the written word when compared to oral propaganda
C. an introduction to a series of essays written by a group of authors about anarchism
D. an introduction to a series of essays written by one author
E. a stand-alone exposition about the author's changing emphasis on oral propaganda over the written word

33. What function does the third paragraph serve in the formation of the author's overall argument?

A. It introduces the author's argument that oral propaganda cannot function on its own, but requires written exposition and encouragement.
B. It allows for consideration of the opposite side of the author's argument to provide balance and insure the author against accusations of bias.
C. It negates the argument made earlier by the author that the written word is limited in how much it can affect the mindset of the individual.
D. It discusses the relationship between the reader and the writer and how this can be manipulated by a skilled author.
E. It acts as a transition from a discussion of the author's youthful and naïve faith in the power of the oral propaganda to a more lasting belief in the power of the written word.

34. The primary purpose of this essay is _____.

A. to lament the loss of oration as an art form and suggest that the written word, when argued convincingly, is the only recourse left to a would-be anarchist trying to bring others into the fold.
B. to compare the benefits of the written and spoken word
C. to demonstrate why orators have such difficulty in convincing an audience to change its opinions
D. to argue in favor of political anarchism
E. to explain the author's transition into writing her arguments, as opposed to offering her opinions in the form of oration

35. The author's point of view in this passage is primarily that _____.

A. When trying to influence people's perspectives and opinions the written word is a much more powerful tool than oral expression.
B. The power of oral propaganda is on the decline as people become more and more resistant against the opinions of others.
C. John Most is an exemplary figure in the propagandist movement, one whose influence the author cannot hope to match.
D. Neither the written word nor oral propaganda can function independently of one another.

E. It is naïve to place one's faith in the power of oral propaganda when people are so apt to ignore what they hear.

36. The author's attitude towards oral propaganda could best be described as _____.

A. disparaging
B. disenchanted
C. supportive
D. uneasy
E. nostalgic

Answer sheet with explanation

1. **Correct Answer:** A biologist noticing trends in a set of collected data, accounting and controlling for extraneous variables, and creating a general model that can be applied to other relevant instances

Explanation: The form of theoretic jurisprudence, according to the author, is one that very closely resembles an empirical science-that is, it draws conclusions based on trends noted from relevant data, with extraneous or distracting factors accounted for or removed, used to create models that predict future results. As such, the most closely analogous case would be the one that follows this pattern, especially the necessary condition that the model be useful for predicting future cases.

2. **Correct Answer:** There is nothing irrelevant to the practice of law.

Explanation: The author states ("The reason why a lawyer does not mention that his client wore a white hat when he made a contract") that there are some details that are irrelevant in making legal arguments. Other responses can be supported by specific statements in the passage (e.g., "It is to make the prophecies easier to be remembered and to be understood that the teachings of the decisions of the past are put into general propositions and gathered into textbooks" and its surrounding context supporting the notion that legal principles are guides to helping predict the outcome of a case).

3. **Correct Answer:** The proper subject of the study of law itself, as opposed to individual laws, is to derive and deduce legal principles from first principles.

Explanation: While it is unlikely that the author would agree with any of the responses, as they either have no relevance to the passage or contradict details of it, the credited response is the one that most nearly contradicts the main idea of the passage: that jurisprudence is concerned not with deriving legal principles from eternal first principles of morality, but with predicting how courts will act in certain situations given past cases and statutes.

4. **Correct Answer:** It is not necessary to learn every single court decision, statute, or legal determination that has been issued in the last 600 years, as the relevent issues are recapitulated and reinterpreted regularly.

Explanation: The final paragraph claims that, while the already overwhelming body of law in its statutes and decisions is growing by the moment at a rate nobody could ever hope to keep up with, mastering every single detail of the centuries-old corpus is not necessary as the main issues are reinterpreted in ways relevent to contemporary society in every generation. The credited response most closely matches this point in its details, capturing not only the overwhelming size of the legal corpus and its inexorable increase, but also the nature of how it is recapitulated in every generation and the practical consequences for legal practice.

5. **Correct Answer:** "We must beware of the pitfall of antiquarianism, and must remember that for our purposes our only interest in the past is for the light it throws upon the present."

Explanation: The author's attitude towards past legal decisions and statutes is one in which this history has its uses for understanding the present, but there are certain limits to its use; as soon as a historical approach ceases to be useful in "explaining a conception or interpreting a rule," it is to be abandoned. Thus, while an understanding of legal history is useful to a degree, it is not to be used to the exclusion of other methods. The credited response is the one that best shows this limited approach to the use of legal history. While some other responses mention history, and, indeed, how present practice can flow from the past, they do not mention the limits that ought to be placed on deference to the past; indeed, the requirement in one response that legal reasoning "follow from the principles of personal and political morality" of past legislators contradicts Holmes's assertion that there are strict limits to the use of history.

6. **Correct Answer:** The law is itself lawful, and the one who understands its first principles can reason to its conclusions.

Explanation: The credited response most closely matches the idea, rejected by the author, that law can be conducted as if by syllogism, proceeding from known premises always and truly via logic to certain conclusions. The picture painted by the author is one in which many factors—history, ethics, society and its changes, and "what is then considered to be convenient"-combine and meld to form the body of law, a sometimes disorderly and not strictly logical body. The other responses, while perhaps not always strictly in agreement with all of the author's nuances and ideas, do not so directly contradict the central thesis of the passage.

7. **Correct Answer:** there is no role for systematic logic in the interpretation of laws

Explanation: While the author does spend the first paragraph attacking the idea that law is a strictly logical discipline, he never says that it is not one in which logical procedures and operations are not to be used-just that their use must be subordinated to experience.

Other responses can be validly extrapolated from specific citations in the text (e.g., "The felt necessities of the time ... should be governed" supporting the idea that laws reflect the societies in which they were enacted), while the idea that there is nothing formally logical in the practice of law cannot.

8. **Correct Answer:** A set of examples used to illustrate an assertion earlier in the passage

Explanation: The passage makes an allusion to a body of examples - the laws of Massachusetts - in order to show through an example how a certain assertion made in the previous paragraph - that law reflects what is convenient at a certain place and time and its present form reflects its past - might be justified; however, it cannot be called a specific example (no particular law of the Commonwealth is referred to, much less how that law is indebted to ancient Europe), nor one that bolsters a premise in an earlier argument. The paragraph does not illustrate procedures being applied, as no specific procedures are being discussed here; nor does it contrast two approaches to the study of any subject, but rather the reasons behind the form and functioning of laws; nor does it make a merely rhetorical contrast.

9. **Correct Answer:** The work of Copernicus was a necessary step for people to be able to think of other worlds as possibly inhabited.

Explanation: The author implies that the Copernican revolution was a necessary first step to people thinking of the Earth as one celestial body among many ("the new [Copernican] conception of [the Earth's] position involves a promotion, since the earth itself is now regarded as a heavenly body of the same order as some of those that shine down upon us"), which was itself a necessary step for people to also think of other celestial bodies as possibly being inhabited. Thus, without the Copernican revolution, it would not have been possible to consider other worlds as potentially being inhabited if the author's assumptions are true.

10. **Correct Answer:** No uninhabited world is the home of intelligent beings.

Explanation: The presence of intelligent beings is a necessary, but not sufficient, condition for a world to be inhabited; however, the passage also implies that the presence of intelligent beings on an inhabited world does not necessarily imply a lack of unintelligent ones as well. While this is most strongly suggested by the description of terrestrial explorers needing to find human beings in addition to plant and animal life, it is not precluded by the logical structure of the argument. The presence of intelligent life does not necessarily exclude the presence of non-intelligent life (A does not imply not-B), even if there is nothing in the passage that suggests that intelligent life requires non-intelligent life.

11. **Correct Answer:** An additional, secondary conclusion that can be derived from the primary conclusion of the passage

Explanation: The final sentence is a secondary conclusion based on one of the implications of the main conclusion of the section. As the primary conclusion states that all inhabited planets must have intelligent life with physical bodies, one may draw the subsequent conclusion that any inhabited planets must, as a necessary condition for these beings, meet certain conditions required by the bodies of living beings. This point is not so much the primary conclusion of the passage as it is an inference drawn from analyzing an assumption implicit in the necessary conditions for supporting certain kinds of life.

12. **Correct Answer:** Reflective and philosophical

Explanation: The author, who spends his first few paragraphs reflecting on the development of humanity's conception of the cosmos, adopts a philosophical point of view, examining the implications of these developments primarily from a metaphysical standpoint. While his tone is not especially emotional or passionate (ruling out many of the more extreme or emotionally charged options, like "witty" or "elegiac"), it is not overly detached and dry, like one would expect from "formal," "didactic," "objective," or "serious" writing.
The balanced, moderate, and reflective tone leads to choosing descriptors that are themselves neither overly intense nor overly removed in describing passion and emotion.

13. **Correct Answer:** As science has progressed, people have wondered if there are other worlds that might be inhabited by creatures like ourselves.

Explanation: The credited response is the only one that addresses the thesis of the passage as a whole, rather than the points of individual paragraphs or sections. While the other responses are supported by the passage, they do not capture the overall aim of the passage as a whole, which is what this particular type of question asks about. There are several parts and subsidiary ideas in this passage to look for in determining the credited response: the advancement of science, the conditions needed for a world to be considered inhabited, and how like human beings the inhabitants of other worlds must be. All of these are present in the correct response.

14. **Correct Answer:** Giving the history of the development of a theory; mentioning a consequence of this development; describing necessary conditions for a state of affairs; drawing conclusions from these conditions

Explanation: The credited response is the only one that describes the rhetorical and logical structure of the passage. The passage begins with a historical overview, before describing the scientific and philosophical consequences of the developments described in that overview. It then lays out the necessary conditions needed for a world to be considered inhabited before extrapolating conclusions from the consequences of these conditions. There is no mention of empirical scientific investigation based on observations, nor are there discussions of theoretical models, eliminating all responses that mention them.

15. Correct Answer: To transition between the historical and metaphysical survey of the opening paragraphs and the logical arguments of the following ones

Explanation: This paragraph is primarily a transition between the first and second sections of the passage. It attempts to connect the historical development of a contemporary problem—the controversy over the plurality of worlds—with some logical arguments that relate to that controversy, which is discussed in later paragraphs. By foreshadowing the eventual conclusion that will be argued for in the next paragraphs (inhabited worlds must contain intelligent creatures with physical bodies), the paragraph shows where the passage will eventually be heading. By mentioning the then-contemporary controversy of the plurality of worlds, it brings the historical sketch into the present, where it may be concluded, and by uniting the history of the first part of the passage and the logical arguments of the second part of the passage, it unites the two modes used in their respective sections and transitions from the one to the other.

16. Correct Answer: The monasteries of Medieval Europe were centers of scientific learning because of their ability to merge religious and scientific inquiry cohesively.

Explanation: Answering this question requires a good deal of inference on your part. Let us tackle this question by eliminating one answer choice at a time. The author's discussions of different philosophers' motivations in the first paragraph suggest that he would certainly agree that "Philosophers' motivations may be classed as either scientific or religious and ethical, or as drawing from both areas." Additionally, although he makes no mention of "organized" religion, we can assume he would be as dismissive of it as he is of religion in general. Similarly, although the author is writing at the beginning of the twentieth century, we can infer from his arguments that he would believe a great deal of the scientific achievement of the last century is down to mankind's increasing neglect for religious motivations. That leaves either "None of these" or "The monasteries of Medieval Europe were centers of scientific learning because of their ability to merge religious and scientific inquiry cohesively." Based on the author's general disdain for the influence of religion on science, it is reasonable to assume he would argue that the monasteries of Medieval Europe achieved their success in science "in spite" of their preoccupation with religion, rather than because of their ability to merge science and religion cohesively.

17. Correct Answer: Impossible

Explanation: This question can be answered quite easily, either through an understanding of context or by understanding the definition of the word "insoluble." In context, the author discusses how philosophers are expected to determine the nature of the universe, and give cause for optimism or pessimism, and how this expectation is misplaced. One could reasonably infer that he believes determining the nature of the universe is "impossible." Also, the author states plainly, "I believe the conception of 'the universe' to be, as its etymology indicates, a mere relic of pre-Copernican astronomy, and I believe the question of optimism and pessimism to be one which the philosopher will regard as outside his scope, except, possibly, to the extent of maintaining that it is insoluble." "Insoluble" means not achievable, or impossible to solve.

18. **Correct Answer:** Hume

Explanation: In the opening paragraph, the author details the different types of philosophical inquiry, and throughout the essay he argues that philosophy grounded in science is significantly more useful than philosophy grounded in religion. He states, "These two groups of motives are, on the one hand, those derived from religion and ethics, and, on the other hand, those derived from science. Plato, Spinoza, and Hegel may be taken as typical of the philosophers whose interests are mainly religious and ethical, while Leibniz, Locke, and Hume may be taken as representatives of the scientific wing. In Aristotle, Descartes, Berkeley, and Kant we find both groups of motives strongly present." In answering this question, we must identify a philosopher who is in the same camp as the author; this is plainly Hume, who is "representative of the scientific wing."

19. **Correct Answer:** While many believe that evolution represents a successful combination of science and ethics, the author would likely disagree with this view.

Explanation: We can figure out the correct answer by considering each answer choice carefully. "Only scientific philosophers are expected to tell us something about the nature of the universe" is incorrect because the passage says, "A philosopher is expected to tell us something about the nature of the universe as a whole," and does not differentiate between scientifically-motivated and religiously-motivated philosophers in describing this expectation. "Scientific results are remarkably useful when applied to the sphere of philosophy" is incorrect because in the fourth paragraph, the author argues that "Much philosophy inspired by science has gone astray through preoccupation with the results momentarily supposed to have been achieved." "A number of philosophers cannot be classed as either being motivated by science or as being motivated by ethics and religion" is incorrect because in the first paragraph, the author claims that "broadly speaking, [philosophers] can be divided into two groups... those derived from religion and ethics, and ... those derived from science." While the author continues by mentioning that certain philosophers fall into both of these groups, no mention is made of a significant number of philosophers falling outside these two groups entirely. "Science has experienced the same sort of setbacks in recent years as religion has during the past" is entirely unsupported by the passage, as at no point does the author compare setbacks experienced by science to setbacks experienced by religion; he blames the first on religious influence and urges the second.
Eliminating all of these answer choices leaves us with the correct answer, "While many believe that evolution represents a successful combination of science and ethics, the author would likely disagree with this view." This answer is supported by the last sentence of paragraph two, "[Herbert Spencer's] ethical preoccupations are what make him value the conception of evolution-that conception in which, as a whole generation has believed, science and morals are to be united in fruitful and indissoluble marriage." We can infer based on the author's view as explained in the rest of the passage that he would not agree that science and morals can be successfully united, as he sees religious and moral influences as hindering scientific philosophical enquiry and the proponents of each camp as "often antagonistic."

20. **Correct Answer:** critical and intolerant

Explanation: Throughout the text, the author rallies against the influence of religion and ethics on science and on philosophical inquiry.
Consider this excerpt: "It is my belief that the ethical and religious motives in spite of the splendidly imaginative systems to which they have given rise have been on the whole a hindrance to the progress of philosophy, and ought now to be consciously thrust aside by those who wish to discover philosophical truth. Science, originally, was entangled in similar motives, and was thereby hindered in its advances." From this quotation, we may determine that the author views religion and its influence negatively.
However, he is never arrogant or mocking in his dismissal; rather, it is more accurate to say he is "critical and intolerant." When determining tone and attitude of an author, be wary of selecting an answer that is overly strong without sufficient evidence to support this conclusion. Authors of well-known essays are rarely completely one-sided or brazen in their attacks, for this generally weakens academic writing.

21. **Correct Answer:** Hostile and non-complementary

Explanation: This question might be answered from an understanding of the whole text, but then there are a couple of different answers that might be reasonably selected, such as "Puzzling and oppositional," "Wanton and pointless," and "Hostile and non-complementary." Instead, it is better to look for a piece of specific evidence to give the best possible answer. Luckily, such a piece of evidence appears early in the introduction when the author states, "When we try to ascertain the motives which have led men to the investigation of philosophical questions, we find that, broadly speaking, they can be divided into two groups, often antagonistic, and leading to very divergent systems. These two groups of motives are, on the one hand, those derived from religion and ethics, and, on the other hand, those derived from science." The author states that the two groups are "antagonistic, and leading to very divergent systems." From "antagonistic" we may derive "hostile," and from "divergent" we may derive "non-complementary."

22. **Correct Answer:** "On the Positive Applications of Scientific Method to Philosophy"

Explanation: When asked to determine the best title for an essay, you are mostly being asked if you understand the primary motivation and thesis of the passage. Many of these answer choices are part of the argument, but only one represents an accurate portrayal of the thesis. The following answer choices are deficient: "On Results-Based and Method-Based Scientific Philosophical Inquiry" is incorrect because it does not convey the author's support of method-based scientific philosophical inquiry whereas another the correct answer does; "In Praise of Herbert Spencer" is incorrect because the author only mentions Spencer in passing, and indeed is as much critical (although in a veiled manner) as he is effusive with praise; "In Defense of Scientific Inquiry and Exploration" is incorrect because it covers only part of the argument and does not transcend the whole of the essay; and "On the Overwhelming Influence of Religion on the Development of Philosophical Thought" is incorrect because this is discussed only in passing to reinforce part of the author's argument against religious motivations. The best answer choice is "On the Positive Applications of Scientific Method to

Philosophy" because it captures the primary motivation of the author, to urge his audience to embrace scientific method in their pursuit of philosophical truth.

23. Correct Answer: Its entanglement with religious and ethical motivations

Explanation: Answering this question requires paying close attention to detail.
In the third paragraph, the author states, "It is my belief that the ethical and religious motives in spite of the splendidly imaginative systems to which they have given rise have been on the whole a hindrance to the progress of philosophy... Science, originally, was entangled in similar motives, and was thereby hindered in its advances." Based on this quotation, we can ascertain quite plainly that science's entanglement with religious and ethical motives has long hindered its progress, in the author's opinion.

24. Correct Answer: a person in a debate reassessing a misconceived subject

Explanation: Of these five choices, the best is "a person in a debate reassessing a misconceived subject." The author is supposedly presenting facts, but they are more opinions than facts as he does not go into any great detail to prove them. He does reassess the general opinion of the barbarians as those who destroyed Rome, so he is initially dealing with a misconceived subject. The analogy of the doctor would be correct if the word "malignant" was replaced with "benign."

25. Correct Answer: Majorian should have been laxer in trying to increase the numbers of his citizens.

Explanation: When addressing Majorian's rules concerning repopulation, the author states that "the means which he employed to accomplish these salutary purposes are of an ambiguous, and perhaps exceptionable, kind." He goes on to list some of the harsh rules instated during Majorian's rule. Perhaps if Majorian had been more lax or easygoing in his rules, the author would be more likely to assent to them. The other answers can be proven false by searching the text. The answer concerning "virtues and principles" is made false by the phrase "the degenerate Romans."

26. Correct Answer: Great buildings go towards making and defining a great culture.

Explanation: The passage argues a great deal about architecture and the city slowly falling into ruin and would suggest that a great culture is defined by its buildings more than its people. The people who destroyed the city are seen as lesser than those who tried to save it. The author does not mention functional buildings, only those we would consider magnificent. The author draws a parallel between building and culture in Majorian, who he cites as a man of "taste and spirit" who seems to be alone in the author's description of those who worked to save the city.

27. **Correct Answer:** During the period in question the quarries sold more stone than in the previous century.

Explanation: The author states quite emphatically that "the monuments of consular, or Imperial, greatness were no longer revered, as the immortal glory of the capital: they were only esteemed as an inexhaustible mine of materials, cheaper, and more convenient than the distant quarry." Whilst some of the other statements would conflict with the author's argument, the one which would be most harmful to the author's conclusions would be that the quarries actually prospered during this time. If the quarries had prospered, then it would suggest that building occurred more often and demolishing to recycle cheap materials did not occur as much.

28. **Correct Answer:** Show that Majorian was striving, beyond reasonable morals, to reinstate Rome's greatness

Explanation: The author quite clearly respects Majorian yet disagrees with the brutality of some of his methods, as he switches between the apologetic tone found in the line "Majorian was anxious to protect the monuments of those ages, in which he would have desired and deserved to live," and the questioning tone of the line "the means which he employed to accomplish these salutary purposes are of an ambiguous, and perhaps exceptionable, kind." So we can only really say that the author is stating the methods with which Majorian was trying to reinstate Rome's greatness and how they were questionable measures from a modern perspective.

29. **Correct Answer:** A statement that the relationship between the reader and writer is as detached as the relationship between speaker and listener.

Explanation: The author states quite plainly that "[t]he relation between the writer and the reader is more intimate," with the comparison being made between writer and reader and speaker and listener.
So, we know that author would be most likely to disagree that the relationship between reader and writer is as detached as the relationship between speaker and listener. You could also attempt to disprove all the incorrect answers. The author laments her own youthful naiveté, so we can assume she would agree with an argument that youthful enthusiasm and certainty is often misplaced. Additionally, the author clearly is in favor of the anarchist movement and praises John Most heavily in the introduction, so we can infer that she would agree with the two statements relating to his subject matter. Finally, the author discusses at length the difficulty faced by an individual who attempts to impact others through spoken word, so we can also infer that she would agree with this statement.

30. **Correct Answer:** The listener will be awoken from his or her apathy.

Explanation: This question simply requires reading in detail and understanding that the word "lethargy" means something very similar to "apathy." The author states, "I came to see that oral propaganda is at best but a means of shaking people from their lethargy: it leaves no lasting impression."

31. **Correct Answer:** The turbulent and emotional young period of an activist's life changes how they approach their work; it can lead to a maturity or abandonment of values depending on the will of the individual to resist change or complete alteration.

Explanation: The German phrase "Sturm und Drang" means something like turbulent, youthful, and emotional period, but you do not need to know this information to answer the question. The specified quotation appears immediately following the author's exclamation, "Oh, for the naivety of youth's enthusiasm! It is the time when the hardest thing seems but child's play. It is the only period in life worthwhile. Alas! This period is but of short duration." This provides the context with which the quotation can be analyzed and inferred to have a similar meaning. The author is saying that in the turbulent period of youth a propagandist (or activist) will undergo changes in opinion and perspective, and that these opinions are subject to maturity or abandonment depending on the individual's ability to resist "vicissitudes." "Vicissitudes" are unwelcome changes.

32. **Correct Answer:** an introduction to a series of essays written by one author

Explanation: The manner in which the author concludes this essay suggests that it is intended to function as an introduction to a larger body of works written by this author, probably on the topic of anarchism. The author states, "It is this certainty that has induced me to gather in one volume my ideas on various topics of individual and social importance. They represent the mental and soul struggles of twenty-one years-the conclusions derived after many changes and inner revisions."

33. **Correct Answer:** It acts as a transition from a discussion of the author's youthful and naïve faith in the power of the oral propaganda to a more lasting belief in the power of the written word.

Explanation: In the first two paragraphs, the author discusses her early experiences with oration as a convincing means of conveying a message to a large group of people; however, from her tone and expressions, we can tell that she believes this faith to be misguided and attributes it distinctly to youthful naiveté. The author begins the third paragraph by stating, "My great faith in the wonder-worker, the spoken word, is no more. I have realized its inadequacy to awaken thought, or even emotion." This seems to demonstrate a renunciation of her previous faith. She continues in the fourth paragraph to state how "[i]t is altogether different with the written mode of human expression." Collectively, this information suggests that the third paragraph functions as a transition.

34. **Correct Answer:** to explain the author's transition into writing her arguments, as opposed to offering her opinions in the form of oration

Explanation: It is true that based on the evidence in this passage, the author would be likely to argue in favor of anarchism. It is also true that the author discusses why orators have such difficulty in convincing an audience to change its opinions, and finally, it is true that the author compares the benefits of the written word to those of the spoken word; however, the primary purpose of this essay is to reveal the reasons and motivations behind the author's own transition from a belief in oration to an emphasis on the written word. Evidence for this can be found most noticeably in the conclusion when the author summarizes her purpose for writing the passage: "The relation between the writer and the reader is more intimate. True, books are only what we want them to be; rather, what we read into them. That we can do so demonstrates the importance of written as against oral expression. It is this certainty which has induced me to gather in one volume my ideas on various topics of individual and social importance."

35. **Correct Answer:** When trying to influence people's perspectives and opinions the written word is a much more powerful tool than oral expression.

Explanation: This question is primarily aimed at determining whether you understand the author's attitude, intentions, and thesis. Two of the answer choices have no evidence whatsoever to support them in the text; these are: "The power of oral propaganda is on the decline as people become more and more resistant against the opinions of others" and "Neither the written word nor oral propaganda can function independently of one another. " Two of the answer choices summarize only a part of the author's point of view and do not capture the primary thesis and intention of the text; these are: "It is naïve to place one's faith in the power of oral propaganda when people are so apt to ignore what they hear" and "John Most is an exemplary figure in the propagandist movement, one whose influence the author cannot hope to match." The only answer choice that matches the thesis, the author's attitude, and her intentions is "When trying to influence people's perspectives and opinions the written word is a much more powerful tool than oral expression." In answering questions about the author's "primary point of view," be careful not to pick an answer that only summarizes the author's secondary or partial opinions.

36. **Correct Answer:** disenchanted

Explanation: From the author's description in the first two paragraphs, it is clear that she once placed great faith and optimism in the power of oral propaganda; however, from the context of the remainder of the essay, it is clear that that faith has evaporated as the author has matured. Therefore, her attitude could best be described as "disenchanted." She certainly could not be described as "supportive," as she spends much of the essay arguing against the power of oral propaganda. "Nostalgic" functions to an extent, as the author is reflecting on past events and thoughts, but "nostalgia" suggests at a positive reflection and this is clearly negative. "Disparaging" is too strong of a word in this instance to accurately convey the whole of the author's attitude, and "uneasy" is too weak of a word, as it suggests merely limited confidence, as opposed to "disenchanted," which suggests a loss of confidence.

Practice Test 4: Science (optional) section

Scientists studied a species of termite and looked at their foraging habitats across the United States. The termite's population in a given tree was measured by the level of decomposition within a tree, due to the termites eating the bark. The experiment also kept track of the level of shade tolerance for each species of tree. For the species of trees in this experiment, shade tolerance fell into two main categorizes- shade tolerant (ST) and intermediate shade (IS). Lastly, they recorded the average amount of rainfall in that given month for the species location being observed. The chart below summarizes the data. Scientists hypothesized that the level of decomposition would be highest in tree species with a higher average rainfall. In addition, they hypothesized that the trees allowing more shade would allow for more termites and, in turn, more decomposition.

	Tsuga canadensin	Morus rubra	Pinus strobus	Acer rubrum	Arbutus menziesii	Quercus lobata	Juniperus scopuloum
Decomposition (in cm)	2.38	3.21	1.01	.970	2.89	1.31	4.03
Shade tolerance	ST	ST	IS	IS	ST	IS	ST
Average rainfall	47.27	50.89	43.26	41.65	46.87	44.98	52.75

1. The relationship between average rainfall and the quantity of termites in a certain tree species is that _____

- o quantities of termites stay the same regardless of rainfall rates.
- o None of the answer choices listed
- o higher rates of rainfall accompany lower quantities of termites.
- o lower rates of rainfall accompany greater quantities of termites.
- o higher rates of rainfall accompany greater quantities of termites.

2. What is the relationship between shade tolerance and the level of decomposition?

- o Tree species with higher shade tolerance have higher levels of decomposition.
- o Tree species with less shade tolerance have higher levels of decomposition.
- o Tree species with higher shade tolerance have lower levels of decomposition.
- o There is not a consistent relationship between shade tolerance and decomposition levels within the tree species studied.
- o The level of decomposition stays the same regardless of shade tolerance.

A scientific experiment is conducted to test if calcium can affect gene regulation. Scientists hypothesize that high levels of calcium would interact with the proteins Cs3 and Gfy, which would increase the transcription of genes F4597 and BC392. The experiment procedure is summarized below.

- Isolate the genes F4597 and BC392.
- Create a vector within yeast cells containing the two genes

- Culture yeast cells
- Grow yeast cells in different growth mediums—one medium lacking calcium (plate A), and one medium with supplemented calcium (plate B)

3. According to the experiment, what data results would support the hypothesis?

  ○ Both Plate A and Plate B show equal F4597 and BC392 gene activity.
  ○ Plate A shows increased F4597 and BC392 gene activity.
  ○ Plate A shows decreased F4597 and BC392 gene activity.
  ○ Neither Plate A nor Plate B show F4597 and BC392 gene activity.
  ○ Plate B shows increased F4597 and BC392 gene activity.

9. What could be changed to strengthen the design of the experiment?

  ○ Nothing could be changed to strengthen the design experiment.
  ○ Looking at just one protein-gene interaction
  ○ Take out the step looking at protein interaction and focus just on the effects of calcium on the F4597 and BC392 gene activity
  ○ Having a control plate
  ○ Use another substance instead of calcium as the independent variable

Sleep plays a vital role in defining the daily activities of virtually all animals. During periods of sleep, the parasympathetic nervous system becomes active and induces a relaxed state in response to increased levels of the hormone melatonin. Despite its ubiquity in the animal kingdom, the purpose of sleep and its role in our daily lives has been disputed by scientists. Two scientists discuss their theories about the purpose of sleep.

Scientist 1
During periods of sleep, animals are able to conserve energy that they would otherwise be spending on unnecessary activity. If an animal's primary food source is most abundant during daylight, it is a waste of precious energy to be moving about at night. For example, many herbivores, such as squirrels, are diurnal (sleep during the night) because their food source is available during the day, while many insectivores, such as bats, are nocturnal (sleep during the day) because their food source is available during the night. Food sources, as an animal's most valuable resource, dictate their sleep cycles. Many animal traits observable today evolved as a result of the supply and demand of food in their natural habitat.

Scientist 2
During waking hours, it is true that the body utilizes large amounts of energy; however, the role of sleep is to restore biological products that were utilized during periods of wakefulness, rather than simply to avoid utilizing energy in the first place. Many types of biological molecules, such as hormones, are released throughout the body while an animal is active. Sleep serves as a period of inactivity, during which the body can manufacture and store a supply of these molecules for future use during the next period of activity. Furthermore, sleep allows the body to repair cellular damages that has accumulated during waking hours. Experimental evidence shows that when animals are deprived of sleep, their immune system

quickly weakens and death rates increase. Sleep is necessary for animals to prevent accumulation of damage and to regenerate crucial biomolecules for daily life.

4. Scientist 1's theory would be most weakened if which of the following were true?

- o   When deprived of sleep, chimpanzees require more food.
- o   Sharks continue to move constantly while sleeping.
- o   Some herbivores are diurnal, while others are nocturnal.
- o   Bees sleep less during spring, when food is abundant.
- o   Desert animals often spend long periods sleeping during the day.

5. Scientist 2's theory would be most weakened if which of the following were true?

- o   Salmon do not require sleep during the mating season.
- o   Cows show decreased melatonin at night.
- o   Hibernating hedgehogs often become sick soon after waking.
- o   Nocturnal mice have low hormone levels in the morning.
- o   Snakes are diurnal because they are cold blooded.

37. The scientists agree on which of the following principles:

- o   Animals use large amounts of energy while awake.
- o   Animals spend the most time searching for food while awake.
- o   Animals have evolved the need for sleep based on their diet.
- o   Animals will die more easily if they do not sleep.
- o   Animals accumulate biological damage while awake.

38. Which of the following best describes how the scientists view the role of sleep?

- o   Scientist 1: conserve energy; Scientist 2: restore the body
- o   Scientist 1: regenerate biomolecules; Scientist 2: restore the body
- o   Scientist 1: conserve energy; Scientist 2: resource availability
- o   Scientist 1: eliminate wastes; Scientist 2: restore the body
- o   Scientist 1: restore the body; Scientist 2: regenerate biomolecules

A group of scientists wanted to test the effects of Nitra-Grow, a chemical additive that can be given to plants to help them grow. 3 test groups of plants were given all the same time of sunlight, the same type of soil, and the same amount of water. Plant A was given no extra chemicals. Plant B was given 5g of Nitra-Grow. Plant C was given 5g of Ammonia to see if Nitra-Grow worked any better than a basic nitrogen-based household product. The plants are then measured on 5 consecutive days to find their average height (in cm).

DAY	Height Plant A (cm)	Height Plant B (cm)	Height Plant C (cm)
1	1.2	1.2	1.2
2	1.4	1.4	1.2
3	1.6	1.8	1.3
4	1.8	2.4	1.3
5	2.0	2.6	1.4

6. Suppose that the scientists repeated the experiment with Plant D. Plant D was given 15g of Nitro-Grow and 15g of Ammonia. What would be the expected results?

- ○ Plant D would perform the best out of all plants.
- ○ Plant D would perform better than Plant C, but worse than the other two.
- ○ Plant D would perform better than Plant A, but worse than the other two.
- ○ There is not enough information to determine how well the plant will perform.

7. What is the general relationship between plant height and the amount of days?

- ○ As the plant height increases, the time increases.
- ○ There is no relationship between time and height of the plants.
- ○ As the plant height increases, the time decreases.
- ○ As time increases, the plant height increases, then decreases.
- ○ As time increases, the plant height increases.

8. What is the dependent variable?

- ○ Day of measurement
- ○ Type of soil
- ○ Type of chemical added
- ○ Height of the plant

34. On Day 7, what would be plant A's approximate height?

- ○ 2.2cm
- ○ 2.4cm
- ○ An approximate answer cannot be made.
- ○ 2.9cm
- ○ 2.0cm

The significant increase in atmospheric carbon dioxide since pre-industrial levels can be seen in the world's oceans which absorb the CO_2 and in turn undergo changes in chemistry. The consequences of increased CO_2 include acidification of seawater and a decrease in carbonate ion ($CO_3{}^{2-}$) concentration.

Changes in seawater chemistry affect marine organisms. The early life stages of invertebrates, such as squid, may be particularly vulnerable to changes in carbon dioxide levels. Acting as both predator and prey, squid are a significant component of marine ecosystems.   For example, fish and sea birds, such as tuna and albatross, are dependent on squid as a source of prey. Furthermore, the fishing industry is impacted by the health of squid populations. California fisheries produce the majority of market squid.

In order to determine how increased levels of carbon dioxide affect the development of squid, eggs were hatched in two different conditions: normal (380 µatm) and elevated (2100 µatm) levels of CO_2. The time to hatch and the size of the larval mantle (the anatomical feature that includes the body wall and fins) were measured and recorded. Two trials were conducted for each carbon dioxide concentration.

	CO_2 concentration	Temperature	pH	Salinity
Trial 1	380 µatm	20.35	7.89	30.518
Trial 2	380 µatm	20.26	7.84	30.600
Trial 1	2100 µatm	20.28	7.29	30.450
Trial 2	2100 µatm	20.33	7.31	30.724

Water chemistry conditions for each trial

	CO_2 concentration	Length (mm)
Trial 1	380 µatm	1.88
Trial 2	380 µatm	1.91
Trial 1	2100 µatm	1.67
Trial 2	2100 µatm	1.75

Average larval mantle lengths

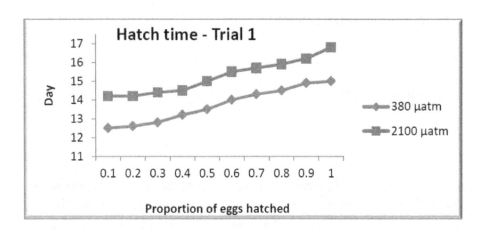

132

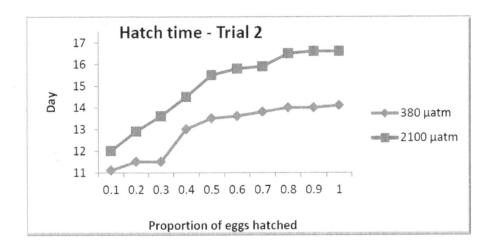

10. Which of the following can be concluded from the passage?

Tuna and albatross populations are directly related
Carbonate ion concentration correlates with ocean temperatures
Atmospheric CO_2 levels correlate with the concentration of CO_2 in the oceans
Carbon dioxide concentration correlates with ocean temperatures

32. The results of this experiment show that _____.

   o   Lower marine pH levels reduce the hatching time of squid
   o   Higher levels of atmospheric carbon dioxide reduce the size of squid
   o   Lower marine pH levels increase the size of squid

Since the early 1900s, there has been a steady increase in the earth's atmospheric temperature, resulting in a phenomenon called "Global Warming." While the steady temperature change has been well documented, the cause of global warming remains controversial.

Scientist 1
Scientist 1 believes that "external forcings" are the cause of increased temperature over the past century. "External forcings" can direct the change in temperature over thousands of years. One example of an external force is variation in the earth's orbit around the sun. The earth orbital cycle lasts 26,000 years and causes general trends in warming and cooling.

Scientist 2
Scientist 2 believes that global warming is a man-made phenomenon due to an increase in greenhouse gases such as carbon dioxide or methane. Greenhouse gases have a natural warming effect, however, an increase in the amount of atmospheric greenhouse gases many enhance that effect. Since 1750, the concentration of carbon dioxide has increased 36 percent while the amount of atmospheric methane has increased 148 percent.

11. Summarize the differences between the scientists' theories.

- Scientist 1 does not believe there has been a significant change in global temperatures while scientist 2 does.
- Scientist 1 thinks global warming is a naturally occurring phenomenon while Scientist 2 believes man is responsible.
- Scientist 1 believes there is no harm in global warming while Scientist 2 believes global warming will be catastrophic.
- Scientist 1 believes a global cooling cycle will occur soon while Scientist 2 does not.

12. What data would support Scientist 1's theory?

- A diagram of the earth's orbital variances
- A chart depicting the average atmospheric temperature each year for the past century
- A chart depicting the number of minutes of daylight experienced at a particular location on June 21st each year
- A chart depicting the average atmospheric temperature every 100 years for the past 50,000 years

13. Assume that both Scientist 1 and Scientist 2 were correct. How would temperature change over the next 20,000 years?

- There would be an increase in atmospheric temperature, however, the rate of increase would change depending on variances in the earth's orbit.
- The average atmospheric temperature will continue to rise at a constant rate.
- The average atmospheric temperature will increase and decrease in a cyclical manner.
- The temperatures in the summers will be hotter while the temperatures in the winter will be cooler.

14.

What is a potential cause for an increase in greenhouse gases since 1750?

- Production of greenhouse gases during the industrial revolution and population growth
- An increase in gas released from melting ice caps
- An increase in chlorofluorocarbons resulting in depletion of the ozone layer
- An increase in the number of plants producing carbon dioxide

15. In the year 2150, the United Nations institutes a global limit on the production of greenhouse gases. The average atmospheric temperature continues to increase, although the rate of increase is less than it was before 2150. Does this invalidate the theory proposed by Scientist 2? Why or why not?

- Yes; If Scientist 2's theory was correct; the atmospheric temperature would not continue to rise.
- No; Increased population may have indirect effects on the concentration of greenhouse gases that cannot be regulated.
- No; A limitation on the production of greenhouses gases will not have an effect on global warming.
- Yes; Limiting greenhouse gas production does not solve the issue of global warming.

- Higher levels of marine carbon dioxide reduce the size of tuna

33. What data supports Scientist 2's theory?

- A graph depicting a negative correlation between the concentration of greenhouse gases and average atmospheric temperature
- A graph depicting a negative correlation between the number of humans on earth and the average atmospheric temperature
- A graph depicting a positive correlation between the concentration of greenhouse gases and average atmospheric temperature
- A graph depicting a positive correlation between the number of humans on earth and the average atmospheric temperature

The chart below depicts the average rainfall by location on the Earth. Zero degrees latitude corresponds to the equator. Positive latitudes are north of the equator, while negative latitudes are south of the equator. A latitude with a magnitude of 90 degrees correlates with one of Earth's poles.

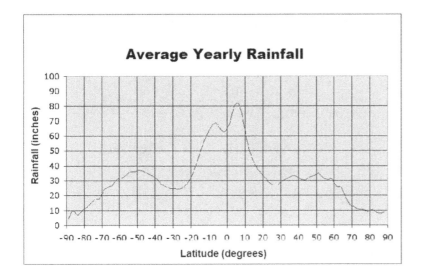

16. Which best describes the rainfall trend between thirty and sixty degrees latitude?

- Rainfall is approximately equal for these latitudes
- Rainfall increases as latitude increases
- Rainfall decreases as latitude increases
- None of these

17. Which of the following best describes the rainfall trend shown in the graph?

- Rainfall is greatest near the equator and least at Earth's poles
- Rainfall is greatest in the Northern hemisphere
- Peak rainfall occurs at about −10 degrees

- o Rainfall is greatest at Earth's poles and declines gradually as latitudes approach 0 degrees

18. Which latitude(s) experience(s) an average rainfall of 35 inches?

- o −55 degrees, −20 degrees and 20 degrees
- o −20 degrees and 20 degrees
- o −55 degrees and 20 degrees
- o −55 degrees

19. The Tropic of Capricorn is about 23.5 degrees south of the equator. Approximately how many more inches of rain does this latitude experience than the North Pole?

- o 25 inches
- o 15 inches
- o 20 inches
- o 10 inches

Laura is performing an experiment with a 5kg weight tied to a 3m rope tied to the ceiling as shown:

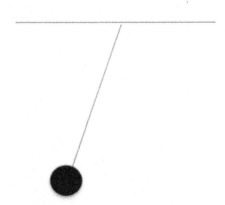

Laura drops the weight and allows it to swing freely. She measures how long it takes for the weight to return to its original position (assume no forces outside of gravity are acting upon the pendulum). This is also called one oscillation.

Experiment 1:
Laura created the following table for her first measurement of the pendulum's oscillations.

Number of oscillations	1	2	3
Length of time	3.474	6.949	10.424

Experiment 2:

Laura performed the experiment again, this time using a 6kg weight.

Number of oscillations	1	2	3
Length of time	3.474	6.949	10.424

Experiment 3:
Laura performed the experiment again, this time using a 3kg weight and a 5m rope.

Number of oscillations	1	2	3
Length of time	4.486	8.972	13.457

20. If Laura stopped experiment 3 after 10 seconds, how many oscillations would the pendulum have gone through?

- o 2
- o 2.5
- o 3
- o 2.23

21. Which of the following statements is a valid conclusion?

- o The length of time of each oscillation is directly related to the mass of the weight
- o The length of time of each oscillation is inversely related to the mass of the weight
- o The length of time of each oscillation is directly related to the length of the rope
- o The length of time of each oscillation is inversely related to the length of the rope

22. Jerry reads about this experiment, and attempts to recreate the experiment at home. He observes that when he lets go of the pendulum, it never reaches its original height. It gets close, but never fully reaches it. Why?

- o Jerry is using the wrong length of rope.
- o Jerry did not tie the pendulum to the ceiling.
- o Jerry is using the wrong weight.
- o External forces acting on the pendulum.

23. How long would 4 oscillations be, using the 3m rope and the 6kg weight?

- o 2.565
- o 13.896
- o 12.566
- o 53.828

24. How much longer does each oscillation in experiment 3 take in comparison to experiment 1?

- o 1.012
- o 0.682
- o 1.111
- o 3.14

25. If Laura recreated experiment 3 using a 5m rope and a 20kg weight, how long would 2 oscillations last?

- o 6.729
- o 8.972
- o 35.888
- o 2.243

26. Which of the following could be an equation for the length of time of one oscillation in experiment 1? (L represents the length of the rope)

- o $\text{Time} = 2\pi \sqrt{\dfrac{L}{9.81}}$

- o $\text{Time} = 2\pi \sqrt{\dfrac{2L}{9.81}}$

- o $\text{Time} = 2\pi \sqrt{\dfrac{mass}{9.81}}$

- o $\text{Time} = 2L\pi \sqrt{9.81}$

27. If Laura recreates experiment 2 using a 300kg weight, how long would each oscillation last?

- o 347.4
- o 3.474
- o 34.74
- o 62.384

28. Laura wants to run a new experiment that has a shorter length of time per oscillation than in experiment 1. Which one of the following would be a good choice for length of rope?

- o 2
- o 3
- o 4
- o 5

29. In experiment 3, how long would 2.5 oscillations last?

- o 13.457

- 13.5
- 16.5
- 8.5
- 11.215

30. If Laura recreated experiment 1 using a 10kg weight, how long would 2 oscillations last?

- 10.212
- 13.898
- 8.972
- 6.949
- 31.416

31. If Laura created a new experiment (experiment 4) and used a 3kg mass and a 6m rope, how long would one oscillation likely be?

- 4.2
- 4.914
- 4.486
- 10.123

The table shows measurements for tumor size growth over time within three different possible treatment methods. Each tumor was first documented at an initial size of 2 inches. Every month each tumor was measured, for a total of five measurements of each tumor.

Chemotherapy	No treatment	Surgery and Chemotherapy
2 inches	2 inches	2 inches
2.1 inches	3 inches	.05 inches
1.8 inches	5 inches	.09 inches
1.4 inches	7 inches	.05 inches
1 inch	9 inches	.03 inches

35. What conclusion CANNOT be reached based on the data shown above?

- All three tumors started being observed when they were 2 inches in size.
- None of these conclusions can be reached based on the data above.
- All of these conclusions can be reached based on the data above.
- Each tumor was measured 5 times.
- All three tumors observed grew at the same rate.

The chart shows the height growth of three different plant species after a period of 2 weeks. Each plant species was grown in 4 different soil mediums. All the plants were grown in the same environment with equal amounts of light, water, and oxygen.

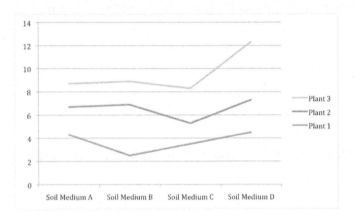

36. What could be added to this experiment to improve the data representation?

   o The Y-axis on the chart should be labeled.
   o The chart should have a title.
   o All of the options listed would improve the data representation.
   o A supplemental chart listing the soil composition breakdown for each soil medium would be helpful.
   o The data would be better represented with "Type of Plant" on the X-axis with four points above for each growth medium.

39. What factor would weaken the design of this experiment?

   o Plant height growth was measured by a computer program.
   o The water used by the plants had mineral levels tested throughout the experiment.
   o Plant 1 requires lighter than Plant 2 and Plant 3 in order to reach maximum growth.
   o All three plants require equal amounts of oxygen and water.
   o All four mediums contain different soil nutrients.

40. Based on the chart, soil Medium C has what effect on plant growth?

   o Soil Medium C is beneficial for Plant 1, but has negative effects on Plant 2 and Plant 3.
   o Soil Medium C has a negative effect on the height growth of all three plants.
   o Soil Medium C does not seem to have a noticeable effect on Plant 1, but has a beneficial effect on Plant 2 and Plant 3.
   o Soil Medium C is beneficial for Plant 2, but detrimental for Plant 1 and Plant 3.
   o Soil Medium C is beneficial for all three plant types.

Answer sheet with explanation

1. **Correct Answer:** higher rates of rainfall accompany greater quantities of termites.

Explanation: The tree species with the highest average rainfall (Morus rubra, Juniperus scopulorum, and Tsuga canadensis) have the highest level of decomposition (3.21, 4.03, and 2.38.) Remember that the experiment uses the level of decomposition as a rough estimation of termite population.

2. **Correct Answer:** Tree species with higher shade tolerance have higher levels of decomposition.

Explanation: According to the chart, the species with a shade tolerance (ST) have levels of decomposition that are higher than species with an intermediate shade tolerance (IS).

3. **Correct Answer:** Plate B shows increased F4597 and BC392 gene activity.

Explanation: To support the hypothesis, the data would need to show that calcium increased the gene activity. Plate B has the supplemented calcium growth medium; therefore, increased gene activity in those plates would support the hypothesis.

4. **Correct Answer:** Sharks continue to move constantly while sleeping.

Explanation: The answer is "Sharks continue to move constantly while sleeping" because Scientist 1 argues that one reason we sleep is because moving around at night wastes energy. Thus, we sleep to conserve energy. If sharks expend energy even while sleeping, this would contradict Scientist 1.
When deprived of sleep, chimpanzees would expend more energy at night and require more, not less, food. During spring, when food for bees is abundant, the bees would be able to gain more energy and sleep less, not more.

5. **Correct Answer:** Hibernating hedgehogs often become sick soon after waking.

Explanation: Scientist 2 claims that animals get sick more easily (have a weakened immune system) when they are deprived of sleep.
Thus, if animals frequently get sick after long periods of sleep, it would contradict Scientist 2's claim. "Hibernating hedgehogs often become sick soon after waking" is the correct answer. Nocturnal mice would have low hormone levels in the morning, according to Scientist 2's theory, and would then replenish those hormones while they sleep during the day. If cows show decreased melatonin at night, it would contradict the facts listed about melatonin at the beginning of the passage, but would not directly conflict with Scientist 2.

6. **Correct Answer:** There is not enough information to determine how well the plant will perform.

Explanation: There is not enough information. You cannot assume it will perform the best because ultimately, negative effects were proven for Ammonia. There is no study on the combination of effects for both chemicals.

7. **Correct Answer:** As time increases, the plant height increases.

Explanation: As time increases, the heights of all plants increase (except for plant B on day 6). The day doesn't change just because the plants grow.

8. **Correct Answer:** Height of the plant

Explanation: Answer, is the height of the plant. The Height of the plant DEPENDS on what type of chemical was being added to the plant.
(The type of chemical added is the independent variable, because the scientist controlled what chemical went in each plant).

9. **Correct Answer:** Having a control plate

Explanation: Having a control plate would allow the researchers to know the vectors were done correctly, and that the yeast cells were healthy and capable of growing regardless of calcium variability.

10. **Correct Answer:** Atmospheric CO_2 levels correlate with the concentration of CO_2 in the oceans

Explanation: Looking at the information given, the only conclusion that can be drawn is that atmospheric carbon dioxide levels correlate with ocean carbon dioxide levels. This is evident from the first sentence of the passage: "The significant increase in atmosphere carbon dioxide since pre-industrial levels can be seen in the world's oceans which absorb the CO_2 and in turn undergo changes in chemistry."

11. **Correct Answer:** Scientist 1 thinks global warming is a naturally occurring phenomenon while Scientist 2 believes man is responsible.

Explanation: Both scientists acknowledge that global warming has occurred over the past century, however, scientist 1 believes global warming is a natural part of the earth's orbital variances while scientist 2 believes that man has contributed to the increase in temperatures.

12. **Correct Answer:** A chart depicting the average atmospheric temperature every 100 years for the past 50,000 years

Explanation: Because the orbital variance changes so slowly (over thousands of years), it will be necessary to compare the average temperature change over a very long period of time. A diagram depicting the orbital variances may be interesting, however, it is not informative for climate change.

13. **Correct Answer:** There would be an increase in atmospheric temperature, however, the rate of increase would change depending on variances in the earth's orbit.

Explanation: A situation in which the temperature continues to increase, but the rate of increase is correlated with changes in the earth's orbit suggests that both scientists are correct. A constant increase in temperature suggests Scientist 2 is correct, while increased and decreased temperature suggests that Scientist 1 is correct.

14. **Correct Answer:** Production of greenhouse gases during the industrial revolution and population growth

Explanation: During the early 1900s, the Industrial Revolution resulted in burning coal for energy, which caused an increase in production of greenhouse gases. Additionally, the increase in population has caused rapid deforestation, reducing the number of plants and trees that consume carbon dioxide. To date, there is no strong link between depletion of the ozone layer and climate change.

15. **Correct Answer:** No; Increased population may have indirect effects on the concentration of greenhouse gases that cannot be regulated.

Explanation: Because there is a modest change in temperature and increased greenhouse gas concentrations cannot be ruled out (through mechanisms such as deforestation), we cannot conclude that Scientist 2's theory was correct.

16. **Correct Answer:** Rainfall is approximately equal for these latitudes

Explanation: Examining the curve of the graph between 20 and 60 degrees, we see that, even though there is slight variation, rainfall hovers around 30 inches. Therefore, we can conclude that these latitudes experiences equal approximate rainfall.

17. **Correct Answer:** Rainfall is greatest near the equator and least at Earth's poles

Explanation: Peak rainfall occurs around the equator (zero degrees). The lowest points occur at the poles (-90 and 90 degrees).

18. **Correct Answer:** −55 degrees, −20 degrees and 20 degrees

Explanation: On the y-axis (Rainfall), locate 35 inches. Find where the curve of the graph intersects this y-coordinate, and find each corresponding x-coordinate. There are three: -55, -20, and 20 degrees. Although 50 degrees also corresponds to a rainfall of about 35 inches, it is not one of the choices.

19. **Correct Answer:** 15 inches

Explanation: To find out the difference in amount of rainfall between these two latitudes, locate -23.5 degrees on the x-axis and find the corresponding amount of rainfall on the y-axis (25 inches). Next, find the latitude of the North Pole (90 degrees) and its corresponding amount of rainfall (10 inches). Finally, subtract the two to find how much more rain the Tropic of Capricorn receives: 25 - 10 = 15 in

20. **Correct Answer:** 2.23

Explanation: Since each oscillation lasts 4.486 seconds, $\frac{10\ seconds}{4.486\ seconds}$ gives us the answer of 2.23 oscillations.

21. **Correct Answer:** The length of time of each oscillation is directly related to the length of the rope

Explanation: In the experiment, the only variable that affects the amount of time of each oscillation is the length of the rope.

22. **Correct Answer:** External forces acting on the pendulum.

Explanation: In the set-up of the problem, it is stated that no forces outside of gravity (such as friction, air resistance, etc.) are acting upon the weight. If those forces also act upon the pendulum, then Jerry's results would be correct.

23. **Correct Answer:** 13.896

Explanation: Based on experiment 2, each oscillation is approximately 3.474 seconds long. 4 oscillations would therefore last approximately 13.896 seconds

24. **Correct Answer:** 1.012

Explanation: To compare how much longer each oscillation in experiment 3 is, simply subtract the two values. 4.486 - 3.474 = 1.012

25. **Correct Answer:** 8.972

Explanation: As shown by comparing experiments 1 and 2, the mass of the weight has no effect upon the time of each oscillation.

26. **Correct Answer:** Time $= 2\pi \sqrt{\dfrac{L}{9.81}}$

Explanation: By plugging in the values from experiment one, the correct answer can be found. Time $= 2\pi \sqrt{\dfrac{L}{9.81}}$

27. **Correct Answer:** 3.474

Explanation: The weight of the object has no effect upon the time of oscillation.

28. **Correct Answer:** 2

Explanation: The shorter the length of rope, the less time each oscillation takes.

29. **Correct Answer:** 11.215

Explanation: Each oscillation lasts 4.486 seconds; therefore, 2.5 oscillations would last 11.215 seconds.

30. **Correct Answer:** 6.949

Explanation: As shown by comparing experiment 1 and 2, the actual mass of the weight has no effect upon how long each oscillation is.

31. **Correct Answer:** 4.914

Explanation: A 6m rope would provide results close to the 5m rope results in experiment 3, but would be slightly bigger. 10 seconds is too long. The other incorrect answers are too small. 4.914 seems most likely.

32. **Correct Answer:** Higher levels of atmospheric carbon dioxide reduce the size of squid

Explanation: The only correct correlation given is that increased carbon dioxide levels reduce the size of the squid. Data for tuna size is not given. As for correlation with pH, lower pH levels correspond to increased hatching time of squid and a decrease in the size of squid.

33. **Correct Answer:** A graph depicting a positive correlation between the concentration of greenhouse gases and average atmospheric temperature

Explanation: Because increased temperature is attributed to an increase in greenhouse gases, a graph depicting a positive correlation between the two is suggestive of a relationship between increased production of greenhouse gases and global warming.

34. **Correct Answer:** 2.4cm

Explanation: The answer is 2.4cm. Every day, plant A increases by a normal rate of 0.2cm per day. Thus adding 0.2 two times to 2.0 will result in 2.4cm.

35. **Correct Answer:** All three tumors observed grew at the same rate.

Explanation: There is not enough information in the data to know that the cancer cells in all three groups grew at the same rate. Cancer cells can grow at different rates depending on size, stage, and other factors.

36. **Correct Answer:** All of the options listed would improve the data representation.

Explanation: All of the options listed would make the data representation better.

37. **Correct Answer:** Animals use large amounts of energy while awake.

Explanation: Each of these answer choices is contained somewhere within the passage; however, most represent the viewpoint of only one scientist. Both scientists agree that animals use large amounts of energy while awake. Scientist 1 bases their theory around this concept, claiming that animals use energy while awake to search for food. Scientist 2 responds by stating "During waking hours, it is true that the body utilizes large amounts of energy. However..."

38. **Correct Answer:** Scientist 1: conserve energy; Scientist 2: restore the body

Explanation: Scientist 1's theory entirely revolves around energy conservation: "During periods of sleep, animals are able to conserve energy." This should immediately eliminate any answer choices in which Scientist 1 focuses on something else.
Scientist 2's theory talks about two topics: restoring biomolecules and repairing damage. "Sleep is necessary for animals to prevent accumulation of damage and to regenerate crucial biomolecules for daily life." The essence of these two components can be combined in the concept of restoring the body.

39. **Correct Answer:** Plant 1 requires lighter than Plant 2 and Plant 3 in order to reach maximum growth.

Explanation: Since the experiment design leaves light constant for all three-plant species, a factor such as a different light preference for one plant species would weaken the control environment for the experiment.

40. **Correct Answer:** Soil Medium C is beneficial for Plant 1, but has negative effects on Plant 2 and Plant 3.

Explanation: Plant 1 is the only plant that had an increased height growth in Medium C. Plant 2 and Plant 3 had decreased height when in Medium C.

Practice Test 5: Full-length simulated exam

To access the full-length simulated exam, click on the link or scan the QR code

CLICK HERE TO DOWNLOAD IT

OR

SCAN THE QR CODE TO DOWNLOAD IT

Practice Test 6: Full-length simulated exam

To access the full-length simulated exam, click on the link or scan the QR code

CLICK HERE TO DOWNLOAD IT

OR

SCAN THE QR CODE TO DOWNLOAD IT

Chapter 8: Test-Day Strategy

Mental preparation

Preparing for test day isn't just about knowing the material; it's equally important to mentally prepare yourself to handle the pressure, manage anxiety, and maintain focus. The stress of taking a high-stakes exam can affect even the most prepared students, leading to mistakes or underperformance. Mental preparation is the key to overcoming these challenges and ensuring that you perform at your best.

Test anxiety is a common experience, often caused by the high stakes of the situation and the fear of failure. Symptoms can range from racing thoughts and difficulty concentrating to physical symptoms like sweating or a rapid heartbeat. It's important to recognize that feeling anxious doesn't mean you aren't prepared; it's a natural reaction to the pressure of performing. However, managing this anxiety is essential to stay focused during the exam.

One of the most effective ways to handle anxiety is to reframe your mindset. Instead of viewing the test as a make-or-break moment, try to see it as an opportunity to show what you know. Remind yourself that the exam is just one part of your overall academic journey, and it does not define your worth. This mental shift can reduce the pressure you feel and help you approach the exam with a clearer mind.

There are several techniques you can use to calm your nerves and prevent anxiety from interfering with your performance:

- Deep Breathing Exercises: When you feel anxious, your breathing may become shallow, which can increase feelings of panic. Practice deep, slow breathing to calm your body and mind. A common method is the 4-7-8 technique: inhale for four seconds, hold your breath for seven seconds, and exhale slowly for eight seconds. This technique activates your body's relaxation response, helping you regain control.

- Visualization: Spend some time before the exam visualizing success. Picture yourself sitting calmly at your desk, working through the questions with confidence. Imagine how good it feels to know the answers and to stay focused throughout the test. Visualization can help reduce anxiety by giving your mind a positive image to focus on, instead of dwelling on fears.

- Progressive Muscle Relaxation: Tension in your body can contribute to feelings of anxiety. Progressive muscle relaxation involves tensing and then relaxing different muscle groups to reduce physical stress. Start by tensing your feet for five seconds, then release. Work your way up the body, focusing on your legs, abdomen, arms, and shoulders.

- Positive Self-Talk: Replace negative thoughts like "I can't do this" with positive affirmations like "I've prepared well" or "I'm capable." Reassuring yourself in this way can help counteract anxiety and keep you in the right mindset during the exam.

In addition to managing anxiety, staying focused is key to performing well. Exams can be mentally exhausting, especially if you're dealing with difficult questions or time pressure. To maintain your concentration throughout, practice these strategies:

- Take Breaks (when allowed): During the test, brief mental breaks can help you reset. Close your eyes for a few seconds, stretch your hands, or take a deep breath. This can clear your mind and allow you to approach the next question with renewed focus.

- Pacing Yourself: Don't spend too long on any one question. If you're stuck, move on and return to it later. This prevents mental fatigue from overthinking one difficult problem and ensures you have enough time to answer the questions you're more confident about.

- Mindfulness: Stay present and focused on the task at hand. If your mind starts to wander or if you begin to worry about your performance, gently bring your attention back to the exam. Practicing mindfulness before the test can help you develop this ability to stay centered.

Mental preparation is just as important as academic preparation for achieving success on test day. By managing anxiety and employing strategies to stay focused, you'll be in the best possible position to perform well. Remember that calmness and confidence come from preparation—both in terms of your knowledge and your mindset. On test day, trust in your abilities and stay focused on the task in front of you, knowing that you've done everything possible to succeed.

What to bring: Paper-based vs. online testing equipment

Whether you opt for paper-based or online testing, knowing what to bring and how to manage your test-taking environment is essential to performing at your best.

Paper-Based Testing: What to Bring

If you're taking the paper-based version of the test, the materials you bring to the testing center will play a crucial role in ensuring a smooth and successful experience. Here's a breakdown of the essentials you'll need:

- Admission Ticket and Photo ID: Always bring a printed copy of your admission ticket, which confirms your registration and allows you entry to the testing center. Your photo ID is equally important, as it verifies your identity. Ensure that your ID meets the requirements of the testing center—typically, a government-issued ID like a driver's license or passport is accepted.

- Number 2 Pencils (with Erasers): The paper-based exam requires the use of number 2 pencils. Mechanical pencils, pens, and any other writing utensils are typically prohibited. Bring at least two or three sharpened pencils to avoid interruptions during the test. Don't forget a good-quality eraser in case you need to change your answers.

- Approved Calculator: For the Math section, a calculator is allowed, but only specific types are approved. Be sure to check the list of acceptable calculators before test day, and bring extra batteries if your calculator is battery-operated. Having a backup calculator isn't a bad idea either, just in case.

- Watch or Timer: Time management is essential, and while many testing centers have clocks, it's a good idea to bring a simple wristwatch to help you keep track of time. Make sure it's not a smartwatch or any device with internet connectivity, as those are prohibited. A basic analog or digital watch will suffice.

- Snacks and Water: Testing can be mentally exhausting, and you'll likely need a break. Pack a snack (such as a granola bar) and water, but note that you can only consume them during scheduled breaks outside the testing room. Stay hydrated and energized during those short pauses.

- Comfortable Clothing: Testing centers can sometimes have unpredictable temperatures. Dress in layers so you can easily adjust to the room's climate without feeling too hot or too cold.

Online Testing: What to Prepare

Online testing has become increasingly popular, but it requires different preparations than paper-based testing. Here's what you need to consider:

- Device Check: You'll need to take the test on a computer or laptop. It's crucial to ensure your device meets the technical requirements set by the testing platform, such as having the right operating system, browser, and internet connection. The testing organization usually provides guidelines or software to test your system compatibility ahead of time.

- Reliable Internet Connection: A stable and fast internet connection is vital for online testing. Ensure you're connected to a network that won't drop out during the exam. If possible, use a wired connection to avoid any disruptions that may occur with Wi-Fi.

- Quiet Testing Space: Unlike a traditional testing center, the responsibility to create a distraction-free environment falls on you for online tests. Find a quiet room with minimal interruptions. Inform family members or housemates of your testing schedule so they can avoid disturbing you.

- Backup Equipment: Have a backup plan for your device or internet. If something goes wrong during the exam, being prepared with a backup computer or knowing where you can quickly switch to another internet connection can save precious time and prevent unnecessary stress.

- Headphones or Earplugs: Depending on the rules of your specific online test, you may be allowed to use headphones to help focus. However, confirm this with the testing guidelines, as some platforms may restrict their use. Alternatively, earplugs can help minimize background noise if you're unable to control the surrounding environment fully.

- Calculator and Scratch Paper: Similar to the paper-based exam, certain sections allow calculators, so have your approved calculator ready. Additionally, check the rules about whether scratch paper is allowed. If it's permitted, ensure you have enough paper and a reliable pen or pencil.

Technical Support: If you're testing online, make sure you know how to access technical support in case anything goes wrong. Some platforms provide immediate assistance if you experience issues during the test.

Practice with Your Setup: Before test day, do a dry run with all your equipment, especially for online testing. Set up your space, test your internet connection, and practice using any necessary software or testing platforms.

Whether you're testing on paper or online, being well-prepared with the right equipment will set you up for a smoother test-taking experience. Take the time to ensure you've packed or arranged everything in advance so that on test day, you can focus on the content and perform at your best without unnecessary stress or distractions.

Test center tips: Staying calm and maximizing focus

Test day can be a nerve-wracking experience, but managing your mental state and staying focused is crucial to maximizing performance. Here are key strategies for staying calm and maintaining concentration at the test center, ensuring that you are fully prepared for a smooth and successful exam day.

Arriving at the test center well ahead of time can help set a calm tone for the day. Rushing or arriving late can increase stress, so plan to arrive at least 30 minutes early. This gives you ample time to check in, settle down, and acclimate to the environment. Knowing that you're not pressed for time can prevent anxiety from building up right before the test.

Once you arrive, take a moment to familiarize yourself with the testing room. This could mean locating the nearest bathroom for breaks, ensuring that you have a clear line of sight to a clock if one is available, or simply finding a seat where you feel comfortable and free of distractions. Being in control of your environment can help you feel grounded and ready to focus on the task at hand.

No matter how prepared you are, test day nerves are common. A great way to mitigate these nerves is to practice deep breathing. When anxiety strikes, your breathing tends to become shallow, which can increase feelings of panic. Controlled breathing exercises help slow down your heart rate and bring a sense of calm. Before the test starts, practice inhaling slowly for four counts, holding your breath for seven counts, and exhaling for eight counts. This helps clear your mind and bring focus back to the moment.

Additionally, if you feel tension building during the exam, try progressive muscle relaxation. Starting from your feet and working upwards, tense and then release each muscle group for a few seconds. This technique can be done discreetly during the test and helps reduce physical stress that might otherwise distract you.

One of the most important aspects of staying focused is being mindful. During a long test, it's easy for your mind to wander, especially if you get stuck on a difficult question. When you notice your thoughts drifting, gently bring your attention back to the task at hand. Don't dwell on a question you can't immediately answer—flag it and return to it later. Staying present in each moment of the test will help you conserve mental energy and maintain a consistent pace.

Moreover, maintain a positive attitude throughout the exam. It's natural to encounter a few challenging questions, but don't let them derail your focus. Remind yourself that you've prepared for this and that moving through the exam steadily is the best approach. Each question you complete successfully builds momentum, keeping you motivated and focused.

If your test has scheduled breaks, use them to reset both mentally and physically. Stand up, stretch, and move around to get your blood flowing. Taking a few minutes to disconnect from the test can help clear mental fatigue and improve focus when you return to the exam. During breaks, avoid obsessing over any questions you've completed. Instead, use the time to relax and refocus for the next section.

Snacks and water during breaks can also help. Make sure you bring healthy snacks that won't weigh you down but provide enough energy to sustain focus. Hydration is essential for maintaining concentration, so drink water during your break to stay alert.

It's easy to feel overwhelmed in a high-stakes testing environment, but it's important to keep the test in perspective. Remember that it's just one part of the overall admissions process, and your performance in this one exam doesn't define you or your future success. Keeping a healthy, balanced mindset helps alleviate pressure and can lead to better performance.

Avoid negative self-talk such as "I can't do this" or "I'm going to fail." Replace these thoughts with affirmations like "I've prepared well," "I know this material," or "I can do my best." This shift in mindset can drastically improve your approach to the test, fostering a calm and focused attitude.

Test day success isn't just about what you've studied but also about how well you manage your mental and emotional state. By preparing your environment, practicing relaxation techniques, staying mindful, and maintaining a positive outlook, you'll be in the best position to handle the pressures of the test center and achieve your desired results. Staying calm and focused allows you to tackle each question methodically, ensuring that all your hard work and preparation pays off.

How to tackle uncertain questions without losing time

Handling uncertain questions efficiently is a critical skill for performing well on test day. Uncertainty is inevitable, especially when dealing with challenging or unfamiliar material, but it's essential to minimize the impact these questions have on your overall performance and time management. Here are several strategies to help you tackle these uncertain moments without losing time or momentum during the exam.

One of the best ways to handle uncertain questions is to trust your instincts. Often, your first guess is based on the knowledge you've accumulated through studying, even if you aren't consciously aware of it. Overthinking an answer can lead you to second-guess yourself and waste valuable time. Studies have shown that when students change their answers, they are more likely to switch from a correct answer to an incorrect one. So, when in doubt, go with your gut and move on.

When faced with a question you're unsure about, a reliable method is the process of elimination. Start by discarding any answer choices that are clearly incorrect or irrelevant. Even if you're not confident in your knowledge of the correct answer, eliminating options narrows the field and increases your chances of making an educated guess. For example, if you can reduce a four-option multiple-choice question to two possible answers, your chances of guessing correctly increase to 50%, significantly improving your odds.

One of the biggest time-wasters during exams is spending too much time on a single difficult question. If you encounter a question you can't answer quickly, don't hesitate to skip it and return to it later. Mark it so that you can easily identify it when you go back, but don't let it slow your progress. By moving on, you ensure that you have enough time to answer questions you know, rather than spending an excessive amount of time on one uncertain question. This approach helps keep your pace steady and reduces the risk of running out of time for easier questions later.

If you've eliminated some answer choices and are still unsure, make an educated guess rather than leaving the question unanswered. There's no penalty for guessing, so it's better to take a chance on getting the question right than leaving it blank. In situations where you're down to two answer choices, try to recall any related knowledge that might help you make the best possible guess.

Additionally, certain patterns can help you make a more informed guess. For example, if the question asks for a factual answer (like in math or science), numerical answers that are extremely high or low may be less likely to be correct. In contrast, answers that are moderate or average often have a higher probability of being correct.

It's easy to feel anxious when you encounter a question you don't know the answer to, but allowing that anxiety to build will only hinder your performance. Practice deep breathing techniques and remind yourself that it's okay to not know every answer. Keeping a calm, focused mindset ensures that you don't let one difficult question affect the rest of your test. If you stay composed, you'll be better equipped to return to uncertain questions later with a fresh perspective.

Once you've completed the easier questions, return to the ones you marked for review. With the pressure of finishing the bulk of the test behind you, you can take a more thoughtful approach to these uncertain questions. Sometimes, the process of working through other questions jogs your memory, and you may find that you suddenly recall information that can help you solve the uncertain questions.

Uncertainty during an exam is unavoidable, but by using strategies like trusting your instincts, eliminating incorrect answers, skipping difficult questions, and making educated guesses, you can prevent these moments from disrupting your overall performance. Staying calm and composed ensures that you approach the test methodically, maximizing your chances of success. These techniques will help you manage your time effectively and give you the best opportunity to excel.

Chapter 9: Post-Test Reflection and Next Steps

Understanding your ACT score report

After you've completed the test, one of the most important next steps is to thoroughly understand your score report. The score report provides valuable insights into your performance and helps guide your decision-making process, whether you're satisfied with your scores or considering a retake. Here's a detailed breakdown of how to interpret the new ACT score report, especially as the format evolves.

The most prominent feature of your score report is the Composite score. This score is the average of your scores from the English, reading, and math sections, each of which is scored on a 1–36 scale. This number represents your overall performance on the core sections and is the primary score that colleges will look at when considering your application. For example, if you score a 28 in English, a 30 in reading, and a 32 in math, your Composite score would be 30.

This Composite score is significant because it's a quick measure of your academic readiness across these key areas. Colleges often use it as a benchmark when comparing applicants, and higher scores can open up more competitive opportunities for scholarships and admissions. However, it's important to remember that different institutions place different levels of importance on the Composite score, so make sure to check the specific requirements of the colleges you're applying to.

Alongside your Composite score, each of the core sections—English, reading, and math—will have its own score ranging from 1 to 36. These section scores provide a more detailed look at your strengths and weaknesses. For example, you may perform better in math than in reading, which can give you a clear indication of where to focus any additional study or improvement efforts if you're considering a retake.

Each section score also comes with reporting categories that further break down your performance. These categories highlight how well you did on specific types of questions within each subject. In the English section, for instance, you might see categories like Usage/Mechanics or Rhetorical Skills. This level of detail is incredibly useful in identifying which skills are strong and which need more work, especially if you plan to focus on improving in a specific area.

If you opted to take the Science section, you'll notice that it is scored separately from the Composite score. The science score will also range from 1 to 36, but it does not contribute to the overall Composite score that combines English, reading, and math. The science section score stands alone and is provided for those who want to demonstrate their proficiency in scientific reasoning, which may be important for students applying to STEM programs.

For students who take the science test, colleges will see this separate score, but they will not receive a Composite score that includes it. This allows students the flexibility to showcase their abilities in science without it affecting their core academic score. This change makes it easier to tailor your test-taking strategy based on your college goals. For example, if you're applying to a liberal arts program, the science score might be less relevant, while a student applying to an engineering program may benefit from having a strong science score.

Another critical part of the score report is your percentile ranking, which indicates how your scores compare to other test-takers. For example, if you're in the 75th percentile, it means you scored better than 75% of students who took the test. This metric helps put your performance into context on a national scale and can give you a sense of how competitive your scores are for college admissions.

Your score report will also include college readiness benchmarks. These are predefined scores that suggest whether you are academically prepared for first-year college courses in areas like English composition, algebra, and biology. Meeting or exceeding these benchmarks is a strong indication of your readiness for college-level work, but falling short in any area may indicate that you need to focus on improving in that subject before entering college.

Once you've reviewed your score report, the next step is deciding what to do with this information. If your scores meet your expectations and align with the requirements of the colleges you're applying to, you can confidently move forward with your applications. However, if your scores are lower than you hoped, consider whether it's worth retaking the test. Your score report provides valuable insights into where you can improve, helping you tailor your study plan and boost your performance on a second attempt.

Understanding your score report is key to making informed decisions about your college applications or future testing strategies. By focusing on the Composite score, section scores, and optional science score, you can gain a full picture of your academic strengths and areas for improvement, giving you the tools to move forward confidently.

Should you retake the ACT? How to decide

Deciding whether to retake the exam can be a challenging decision, but it's crucial to consider several key factors before making your choice. Retaking the test might be the right move if you feel you underperformed or if you're aiming for more competitive college programs. However, it's equally important to evaluate if your score already aligns with the requirements of the schools on your list or if retaking the test could actually result in a lower score. Here's a breakdown of how to make an informed decision.

Step 1: Evaluate Your Current Score:

The first step in determining whether to retake the test is to evaluate your current score in comparison to the average scores of admitted students at your target colleges. Start by researching the median ACT scores for your preferred schools. If your score falls below the average range, especially in competitive programs, retaking the test may improve your chances of admission.

However, if your score is within or above the average range of accepted applicants, you may not need to retake the exam. Many colleges accept a wide range of scores, and as long as your score aligns with their expectations, it may be better to focus your efforts on other parts of your application, such as essays, extracurriculars, and recommendations.

Step 2: Reflect on Your Test-Day Experience

Another essential factor to consider is how you felt during the test. Did you experience test anxiety, or were there distractions that prevented you from performing at your best? If so, you may benefit from retaking the test with better preparation or in a different testing environment. Test-day conditions can significantly affect your performance, so if there were issues beyond your control—such as illness, stress, or timing problems—retaking the test could result in a higher score.

Step 3: Consider the Time Investment

Retaking the test requires significant time and effort. Ask yourself if you can realistically dedicate time to test preparation without compromising other important priorities like schoolwork or extracurricular activities. If you're already spread thin, retaking the exam may cause unnecessary stress, which could negatively impact your other responsibilities.

On the other hand, if you believe you can prepare more effectively and are confident in your ability to improve your score, it might be worth the investment. The question becomes whether you can carve out enough time for thorough preparation while still balancing other obligations.

Step 4: Review Score Improvement Potential

Think about how much you could realistically improve your score. If you know exactly where you struggled—whether it was a particular section or time management—there's a good chance you can improve with focused study. For example, you might have struggled with the math section, but after additional practice, feel more confident about improving your score.

However, if your score is already on the higher end, be aware that it can be harder to gain significant improvements. Going from a 28 to a 34, for instance, may require much more effort than improving from a 22 to a 28. Consider using practice tests to gauge how much you've improved since the last exam.

Step 5: Think About College Admissions Strategy

Consider how important your score is in the context of your overall college admissions strategy. If your application is strong in other areas—such as a high GPA, exceptional essays, or meaningful extracurricular involvement—your test score may not need to be perfect. Keep in mind that many colleges are increasingly adopting test-optional policies, which means your test score may not carry as much weight as in previous years.

However, if you're applying to test-required schools or aiming for merit-based scholarships that are tied to high scores, retaking the test might be necessary. Also, some competitive scholarships may have specific test score requirements, which can make improving your score worth the extra effort.

Step 6: Consider Superscoring

Some schools offer superscoring, which combines your highest section scores from different test dates. If your scores in one section were strong but another section was lower, retaking the test with superscoring in mind could help you present your best possible composite score to colleges.

Should You Retake the Exam?

Ultimately, deciding whether to retake the exam depends on a balance of factors: how close your current score is to your target schools' averages, whether you believe you can improve with additional preparation, and how much time and effort you can realistically devote to test prep. If you're confident that retaking the test will result in a meaningful score increase, and that score improvement will enhance your college or scholarship prospects, it may be well worth the effort.

Moving forward with college applications

After receiving your test scores, one of the most crucial steps is moving forward with your college applications. This phase can be both exciting and overwhelming, as it requires careful planning, reflection, and action. Here's a detailed guide on how to strategically approach the application process after receiving your scores.

Step 1: Analyze Your Scores in Context

Before jumping into the application process, the first thing you should do is take a moment to reflect on your test results. Compare your score to the average admitted student scores at your target schools. Many college websites provide the middle 50% range of scores for admitted students, which represents the 25th to 75th percentile of incoming freshmen. If your score falls within or above that range, you can confidently proceed with applying. However, if your score is significantly lower than the average at a particular school, you might want to reconsider applying or find ways to strengthen the other parts of your application, such as your essays, recommendation letters, or extracurricular activities.

Step 2: Narrow Down Your College List

With your scores in hand, you can now refine your college list. Ideally, this list should consist of safety, target, and reach schools. Safety schools are those where your scores and qualifications are above the school's average admitted student. Target schools are those where your scores fall comfortably within the school's middle 50% range. Reach schools are those where your scores may be slightly below the average but where other parts of your application may still make you a competitive candidate.

Keep in mind that while test scores are important, they are not the only factor in the college admissions process. Some schools are test-optional or test-flexible, meaning they do not require test scores, or they allow students to submit different types of standardized tests. Be sure to research the admissions policies of each school on your list to ensure that your scores are being used in a way that enhances your application.

Step 3: Focus on Other Application Components

With your test scores accounted for, it's time to focus on other parts of your application. This includes your personal statement, supplemental essays, recommendation letters, and your extracurricular activities. Your scores give colleges an idea of your academic readiness, but these additional elements showcase your personality, passions, and character. Make sure that your essays reflect your authentic voice and highlight experiences that make you stand out. This is your opportunity to tell admissions committees what you're passionate about and what kind of impact you want to have in college.

When it comes to recommendation letters, select teachers or mentors who can speak to your academic strengths and personal growth. Provide them with any relevant information they might need, such as a resume or a brief description of your accomplishments, to help them write a strong letter on your behalf.

Step 4: Pay Attention to Deadlines and Requirements

Each college has different application deadlines and requirements. Be sure to note whether you are applying through Early Action, Early Decision, or Regular Decision. Early Action and Early Decision deadlines are typically in November, while Regular Decision deadlines are in January or February. If you are retaking your test to improve your score, keep these deadlines in mind so you have ample time to submit updated results if necessary.

Additionally, ensure that you meet all the specific requirements for each school. Some colleges may have unique essay prompts or require specific documents, so make sure you're clear on what each school expects.

Step 5: Consider Financial Aid and Scholarships

Once you've completed your applications, the next step is to focus on financial aid and scholarships. Many merit-based scholarships are directly tied to your test scores, so if your scores are strong, you may qualify for additional financial support. Research scholarships offered by your target schools and consider outside scholarships as well. Make sure to submit the FAFSA (Free Application for Federal Student Aid) as early as possible, as many schools use this form to determine eligibility for need-based financial aid.

Step 6: Follow Up and Stay Organized

As you move forward in the application process, stay organized by creating a timeline of application deadlines, submission confirmations, and follow-up tasks. Many schools provide portals where you can track the status of your application. Make sure to check your email regularly for any updates or additional requirements from the schools you applied to.

The test score is just one piece of your application puzzle. Moving forward with your college applications involves a balanced approach—leveraging your test scores while also ensuring that other components of your application are strong. Be strategic, organized, and reflective as you complete this important process, and remember that each part of your application works together to tell a story about who you are as a student and a person.

APPENDICES

Frequently Asked Questions

1. When should I take the ACT for the first time?

Most students take the ACT for the first time in the spring of their junior year in high school. This timing allows you to retake the exam in the summer or fall of your senior year if you feel the need to improve your score before submitting college applications. However, if you're taking advanced coursework earlier, you may want to test sooner to maximize your familiarity with key content areas.

2. How many times can I take the ACT?

There is no official limit on how many times you can take the ACT. However, students usually take it between 2-3 times. Each time you retake the exam, you can aim to improve your score based on targeted preparation. Be sure to check whether your schools accept superscoring, which allows colleges to combine your highest section scores from different test dates to form a new composite score.

3. Is the Science section required?

No, starting with the 2025 ACT format, the Science section is optional. You can choose to take it if you feel it aligns with your academic strengths or if you're applying to STEM programs that require a science score. Your composite score will only reflect the English, math, and reading sections, while your Science score will be reported separately.

4. How is the new Composite score calculated?

The Composite score in the revised ACT format is the average of the scores from the English, math, and reading sections, all of which are scored on a 1-36 scale. If you choose to take the optional Science section, it will be presented as a separate score and will not impact the Composite score.

5. Can I skip questions on the ACT?

You can skip questions and return to them later, but it's best to answer every question. The ACT does not penalize for guessing, so it's beneficial to make educated guesses on questions you're unsure about. Use elimination strategies to improve your chances of selecting the correct answer.

---

6. What should I bring on test day?

For paper-based testing, bring your admission ticket, a valid photo ID, an approved calculator for the math section, #2 pencils, and a watch (without an alarm) to help keep track of time. For online testing, ensure you bring the necessary identification and follow specific instructions provided by the test center, as they will supply the testing device.

---

7. How important is the ACT for college admissions?

The importance of ACT scores in college admissions varies by school. Some schools require test scores, while others are test-optional, meaning they don't require them but will consider them if submitted. High scores can strengthen your application, especially if you're applying to competitive programs or for merit-based scholarships.

---

8. What if I'm unhappy with my score? Should I retake the ACT?

Retaking the test can be beneficial if your score is below the average for your target colleges or if you think you can improve in specific sections. Use your score report to identify areas for improvement, and focus your study efforts accordingly. However, consider how much time you can devote to preparation and whether other aspects of your application are already strong.

---

9. What is superscoring and how can it help me?

Superscoring involves taking your highest section scores from multiple test dates to create a new composite score. If your colleges accept superscores, this can work to your advantage by showcasing your best performance across different test dates. Check the admissions policies of your target schools to see if they accept superscored ACT results.

---

10. What strategies should I use if I run out of time during the test?

If you find yourself running out of time, it's essential to prioritize high-value questions and make educated guesses on questions you don't have time to fully solve. Since there is no penalty for guessing, you should answer every question, even if it's a guess, to increase your chances of earning points.

---

11. How do I send my scores to colleges?

When registering for the ACT, you can choose up to four colleges to send your scores to for free. After you take the test, you can still send your scores to additional colleges by paying a fee. You can request to send individual test dates or superscores, depending on your preferences and the policies of your target schools.

12. What if I'm applying to schools that are test-optional?

If a school is test-optional, submitting an ACT score is not required, but a strong score can still help bolster your application, particularly if you have strengths in the areas tested by the ACT. It's worth researching how much weight test scores carry at test-optional schools and making your decision accordingly.

13. Can I change my test date after registering?

Yes, you can change your test date, but there may be a fee involved. Be sure to make any changes as early as possible, as availability may be limited closer to the test date. If you can't attend your scheduled test date, you may also be able to reschedule for a future exam.

14. How can I prepare for the optional Writing section?

The Writing section requires you to write an essay that presents your argument on a specific issue. To prepare, practice writing timed essays that focus on clear, organized argumentation, supported by relevant examples. While the Writing section is optional, some schools may require it, so be sure to check the application requirements for your target schools.

15. How soon will I get my ACT scores after taking the test?

Typically, multiple-choice scores are available within two weeks of the test date, but it can take longer during busy periods. If you took the optional Writing section, your writing score is usually released about two weeks after your multiple-choice scores. Keep in mind that these timelines can vary, so check the official website for updates.

16. What if I need accommodations for the ACT due to a disability?

If you have a documented disability, you can apply for testing accommodations such as extended time, additional breaks, or alternate formats (e.g., Braille, large print). You'll need to work with your school and provide supporting documentation. It's important to apply for accommodations well in advance of your test date to ensure approval.

17. How should I decide between taking the ACT or the SAT?

Both the ACT and SAT are accepted by most U.S. colleges, so the choice depends on your personal strengths. The ACT has a faster pace and includes a science section, while the SAT focuses more on evidence-based reading and math. Take a practice test for both to see which format aligns better with your skills and test-taking style.

18. Can I cancel my scores if I feel I did poorly?

No, once you've taken the test, your scores will be reported unless you do not show up for your scheduled exam or decide to void your test at the test center. However, you can choose which test scores to send to colleges. This allows you to control which schools see which scores, and many colleges only consider the highest score if you retake the test.

19. Do I need to study for all four sections equally?

Not necessarily. If your practice tests show that you're stronger in certain sections and weaker in others, you should allocate more time to areas where improvement is needed. It's also important to review high-yield topics that tend to appear frequently on the test to maximize your score.

20. How much do colleges weigh my ACT score compared to other parts of my application?

This varies from college to college. Some schools consider standardized test scores to be an important factor, while others, particularly test-optional schools, may place greater emphasis on GPA, extracurriculars, essays, and letters of recommendation. It's important to research each school's admissions policies to understand how they weigh test scores.

21. Can I take the ACT online, or do I have to take it on paper?

The ACT can be taken either on paper or online, but availability depends on the test center. Not all locations offer the online option, and you'll need to confirm availability during registration. Online testing follows the same format and scoring as the paper-based test.

22. What are some common mistakes students make when preparing for the ACT?

Common mistakes include cramming the night before, not practicing under timed conditions, and focusing too much on one section at the expense of others. Students often underestimate the value of doing full-length practice tests to simulate the test-day experience and improve pacing.

23. How can I manage my time effectively during the test?

It's essential to familiarize yourself with the time limits for each section and practice pacing strategies beforehand. Skip difficult questions and return to them later to avoid wasting time. Practice managing your time with full-length practice exams, and use a watch during the test to monitor how much time you have left.

---

24. Will I lose points for incorrect answers?

No, there is no penalty for incorrect answers on the ACT. This means you should answer every question, even if you have to guess. Educated guessing strategies, such as eliminating obviously wrong answers, can improve your chances of selecting the correct option.

---

25. How should I prepare if I have limited study time before the test?

If time is limited, focus on your weakest areas and review key concepts and high-frequency topics. Take at least one full-length practice test to get familiar with the timing and format of the exam. Prioritize strategies for answering questions efficiently, such as guessing techniques and time management.

---

26. What role does the Writing section play in college admissions?

The Writing section is optional, and its importance varies by college. Some schools require it for admissions, while others don't consider it at all. If you're applying to schools that value writing proficiency or require the Writing section, it's a good idea to take it. Otherwise, you may be able to skip it if it's not required by your target schools.

---

27. What can I do to prepare in the final week before the test?

During the final week, focus on light review of key concepts and formulas rather than learning new material. Take one last full-length practice test if you have time, but avoid cramming or overworking yourself. Ensure you're familiar with the logistics for test day, such as what to bring and what to expect at the testing center.

---

28. What's the best way to deal with test anxiety?

The best way to manage test anxiety is through consistent preparation and practice under test-like conditions. On test day, focus on breathing techniques, staying positive, and taking short mental breaks when needed. Confidence comes from being well-prepared, so use your practice tests as a way to build up familiarity and reduce stress.

Made in the USA
Coppell, TX
17 January 2025